The Tribalization of Europe

T0056577

The Tribalization of Europe

A Defense of Our Liberal Values

Marlene Wind

polity

First published in 2020 by Polity Press

Polity Press
65 Bridge Street
Cambridge CB2 1UR, UK

Polity Press
101 Station Landing
Suite 300
Medford, MA 02155, USA

ISBN-13: 978-1-5095-4167-6
ISBN-13: 978-1-5095-4168-3(pb)

A catalogue record for this book is available from the British Library.

Library of Congress Cataloging-in-Publication Data

Names: Wind, Marlene, 1963- author.
Title: The tribalization of Europe : a defence of our liberal values / Marlene Wind.
Description: Cambridge, UK ; Medford, MA : Polity, 2020. | Includes bibliographical references. | Summary: "An urgent wakeup call on the dangers of the new tribalism in global politics"-- Provided by publisher.
Identifiers: LCCN 2019053013 (print) | LCCN 2019053014 (ebook) | ISBN 9781509541676 (hardback) | ISBN 9781509541683 (paperback) | ISBN 9781509541690 (epub)
Subjects: LCSH: Group identity--Political aspects--Europe. | Identity politics--Europe. | Political culture--Europe. | Liberalism--Europe. | Democracy--Europe. | Europe--Politics and government--21st century.
Classification: LCC JN40 .W56 2020 (print) | LCC JN40 (ebook) | DDC 306.2094--dc23
LC record available at https://lccn.loc.gov/2019053013
LC ebook record available at https://lccn.loc.gov/2019053014

Typeset in 11 on 14pt Sabon LT Pro
by Fakenham Prepress Solutions, Fakenham, Norfolk NR21 8NL
Printed and bound in the UK by CPI Group (UK) Limited, Croydon

For further information on Polity, visit our website: politybooks.com

Contents

Preface   vi

Introduction   1
Imagined Communities and Identity Politics   12
Tribal Thinking and Dreams of Detachment   21
Why Brexit is Just Another Kind of Tribalism   32
The Tribal Shift in Central and Eastern Europe   41
Who Cares About Democracy?   54
Who Are the People?   64
The Purpose of a Constitution   70
Democracy Without Limits?   78
Are Illiberal Democracies Democracies?   94
Why Liberals Are Increasingly on the Defensive,
    but Shouldn't Be   103
Concluding Remarks   110

Notes   114

Preface

> Politics today … is defined less by economic or ideological concerns than by questions of identity.
>
> Francis Fukuyama, *Identity*

The tribalization of politics is a global megatrend in today's world. The election of Donald Trump, the Brexit vote, populist movements like Catalan separatism – together with democratic backsliding in Central and Eastern Europe – are all clear examples of the mechanisms and effects of tribalization. The key tendencies here are anti-globalism and identity politics: putting cultural differences before dialogue, collaboration, and universal liberal values.

This book argues that tribalism is pulling up the drawbridge to the world – and to Europe. And it's not just "the people" who have chosen this avenue. Trump and Brexit have silenced many former defenders of globalism and liberal values because they feel guilty. Guilty that they didn't see what was coming, and guilty that they ignored the desires of those who now want to put up walls. Along with this a new narrative has come to characterize the debate and the media in numerous parts of the Western world: as we did not predict the rebellion and the identity issues, we now have to embrace the anti-globalists by way of apology and reconciliation.

Tribalism is, however, a dangerous road to go down. With it, and with the retreat of liberal voices, we have put democracy itself in danger. In several places – even in Europe – democracy has already surrendered to illiberalism, by eliminating free elections, an independent judiciary, a free and critical press, and closing down those universities that didn't parrot the leaders of the countries which hosted them. In this sense democracy has already died, just without us noticing it. Tribalism is not just about being pro-nation, anti-EU, and an opponent of supranational institutions and conventions. It is in many instances a bigger and more fundamental movement casting aside all insistence on the liberal democratic principles we once cherished and insisted were defining for our time.

By succumbing to the identity politics that we see in many places and by reducing democracy to "the will of the people" without discussing who the people really are (or should be), we are abandoning the rights, ideas, and principles we have fought for since the end of the Second World War. Rights, ideas, and principles that millions of Europeans, Americans, and Canadians as well as people of several other nationalities died for on our behalf.

At a time when (former) defenders of liberal values are increasingly silent, or have even joined the growing chorus of tribalists, this book is a wake-up call. By using clear, empirical examples pointing out the dangers of identity politics and the insidious logic behind it, the book encourages people to stand up for true democracy and rule of law in Europe. Democracy is not just "the will of the people" in simple numerical terms but is also about respecting fundamental values, minorities, a free and critical press, and independent courts.

There are several people I need to thank for helping me write this book. First of all, however, I have to thank Ana Rosa and Dolores Cruz Arroyo from Espasa.es for convincing me that this book just had to be written, after a thorough discussion of democracy, separatism, and Balkanization with Carles Puigdemont and my colleague Professor Christian Rostbøll at Copenhagen University in January 2018. I would also like to thank Professors Carlos Closa and Juan Mayoral for comments, corrections, and constructive criticism, as well as those many colleagues at iCourts and the Department of Political Science at the University of Copenhagen who patiently listened to my many thoughts on the subject of this book. I am also highly indebted to my research assistants Regitze Frederiksen, Louise Solgård Hvass, Amalie Lund Michaelsen, and Caroline Emilie Björkenheim Rebien for tireless work on copy-editing, commenting, and source-searching, and not least to Adrian Nathan West for magnificent language editing. Finally, yet importantly, I want to thank my family for their patience with me on this project. My husband Kristian patiently listened to my arguments and my two sons Carl and Jakob never failed to debate with me and test my arguments. I remain indebted to them for their continuous encouragement and interest.

Introduction

Not so long ago, most Europeans believed that our common destiny was to exist as a Union with no internal borders. Nationalist sentiments, a destructive cold war, and restrictive ideologies had been eradicated and replaced by a united Europe, inclusive rights, values, and dreams held in common.

As the Soviet Union crumbled and the Berlin Wall fell, the large majority envisioned the world becoming a better place, with fewer hindrances to travel, trade, and communication, not more. The protection of basic rights, the rule of law, democracy, and economic prosperity would now flourish in the East just as they had in the West since the Second World War. The vision of Europeans living, working, and marrying across borders, of the unity in diversity that EU treaties speak so warmly about, was finally something that most people actually believed could be accomplished. It encapsulated the idea of a Europe that could and should consist of many different regional identities, with Scots,

Catalans, Bavarians, Lombardians, and Sami living side by side with (and in) established nation-states.

Unity in diversity also suggested that Europeans – despite their ethnic and cultural differences – had acknowledged that only common aspirations for peaceful co-existence and cooperation could heal the wounds caused by forty-four years of division. In such a world, state borders would have become irrelevant. Separatists and secessionists would serve no purpose, and their raison d'être would have vanished. Why would anyone want to leave their mother nation to create small new city-states if borders had become obsolete? With the important – and extremely bloody – exception of the breakup of Yugoslavia in the 1990s, no one imagined that borders and bombastic territorial symbols would reenter the European mind, let alone enjoy a renaissance. When liberal democracy had finally triumphed over repressive competing ideologies, including nationalisms new and old, new attempts to mark boundaries would look old-fashioned, even ridiculous.

In the aftermath of the Cold War, scholars, too, were optimistic, speaking of "A New World order"[1] and the "end of history,"[2] with belief in liberal democracy, the rule of law, human rights, and freedom of speech replacing divisiveness and creating a (global) community without partitions.

In Europe 2004 – only fifteen years after East German border guards opened the Berlin Wall by accident – eight new democracies from the former Soviet bloc embraced these ideals and joined the EU. For many Central and Eastern Europeans, the European Community represented hope for the future and for a better life without repression. They had escaped the tutelage of the Soviet Union and the Iron Curtain, which had cut them off from the free world for so long. For more than forty years, becoming part of a borderless, open, liberal Europe had been an unobtainable dream. Now it was a reality.

* * *

All this now feels like ancient history. What we have witnessed in Europe over the past five, ten, or fifteen years is an entirely different development from the one described above. Many Europeans seem to have given up on their universalist aspirations and are pulling up the drawbridges – returning to the tribe. The rhetoric of "us" and "them" has returned and identity politics is a winning argument in elections and referenda.

According to a prestigious global research project[3] measuring the state of democracy in the world, Europe is the place where liberal democracy has declined most precipitously in recent years. Probably because democracy here had come to be regarded as a given and because we have become incredibly bad at recognizing when important democratic institutions are being gradually undermined. According to the study, as many as *six* European countries can no longer be classified as liberal democracies but should instead be referred to as hybrid regimes or semi-autocracies. These countries may hold elections, but no longer heed those basic principles that have defined us as European democratic polities since the Second World War.

The main question addressed in this book is: are we witnessing a general tribalization of Europe? Or is it sporadic declines that can be reversed? I will try to

Introduction

argue that the answer depends not only on where we look, but also on the extent to which we are willing to face our own demons. What is undoubtable is that the most original, successful, and innovative supra-statist project that the world has known, the European Union, is in trouble. It – and not least the values it represents – needs new defenders. This book is such a defense.

So, what is tribalization? As I understand it, tribalism is a phenomenon in which cultural, ethnic, and nationalist groupings of various sizes and organization emphasize themselves as the "true" tribe, nation, or culture while verbally or in practice excluding named "others" from being a part of the community. At the same time, they strive increasingly to regress from internationalist structures, if not formally then in practice, by no longer recognizing previously adopted laws, conventions, and common ground rules. If tribalization is a long-lasting trend, as much evidence suggests, it could eventually splinter the continent into hundreds of more or less homogeneous enclaves, undermining the Europe we know today. A Voltairean nightmare, as some would call it, recollecting the Holy Roman Empire's resolution and the patchwork of small entities in constant infighting.

Despite the stunning success of European integration over the past six decades, there seems to be an increasing temptation – even among those who consider themselves progressive – to rally around new exclusionary identities rooted in a more or less fundamentalist version of the nation-state or in regional separatist movements. What do these projects have in common? They all represent – despite their differences – a tireless yearning to stand in opposition to neighboring identities. Chasing enemies and creating opponents is clearly far from a new phenomenon, but the regression we are experiencing in Europe in these years is something new. And now the enemies are apparently not just those who do not share your culture, religion, or identity, but also liberal elites, the EU and the liberal values we have jointly cherished since the Second World War.

Tribalization, in the form I address in this book, also has something in common with the term "ethnocentrism." Ethnocentrism is often characterized as the attempt to reinforce one's own identity by disparaging others. William Graham Sumner defines ethnocentrism as "a view of things in which one's own group is the center of everything and all others ... scaled and rated with reference to it."[4] However, tribalization has an extra, almost activist dimension, which is directed outward. It can be said to be a reappearance of a form of cultural fundamentalism, which sustains its momentum through active demonization and distancing from others. It is an ugly mix of generic populism combined with rage against those who *do not* share a particular cultural, linguistic, religious, historical, national, or even ethnic origin. I have chosen to describe it as tribalism insofar as it often draws on exclusionary language and the building of walls and borders (sometimes merely symbolically) to keep the others out. However, the purpose is not to be mistaken. First and foremost, it serves to stiffen up the "tribe" itself while underlining who does and who doesn't belong.

Where Europe was built on the ethos of common values and inclusiveness, the continent is now split into what the British weekly *The Economist* describes as "the new political divide" between "wall-builders and globalists."⁵ Unfortunately, the wall-builders have the upper hand at present, and the globalists are increasingly keeping mum. I will refer here to tribalization and tribalist tendencies as a kind of Balkanization, by which I mean the breaking up of the continent into several distinct (ethnic) enclaves – either literally or as a metaphorical solution to Europe's problems as currently perceived. Leaving historical circumstances aside, the breakup of Yugoslavia and the Dayton Accords were in many ways a defeat of a European ideal: that ethnicity should never take center stage and define who we are. Although sometimes assuming more civilized forms and simulating something quite different, such as with the separatists in Catalonia or among the many extreme Brexiteers, the rhetoric that was so central to the escalation of the conflicts in the Balkans has now come back to haunt us.

The tribal way of being in the world is spreading and regaining popularity in old Europe as well as new. Not only among more or less ignorant voters who get carried away by populist leaders who cynically exploit primitive language (and social media) to create a feeling of exclusive unity. More frighteningly, perhaps, the rhetoric is spreading among established politicians and opinion makers. Tribalism has become *the* new political megatrend and also *the* go-to argument for demonizing the so-called liberal elites who still believe in the merits of a liberal international order, the dissolution of borders, and joint solutions to common challenges.

The ideal and cultivation of a common past are absolutely central to the current tribal discourse. To the extreme Brexiteers as well as the Catalan separatists

and ethnic-nationalists like Hungarian leader Vikor
Orbán, the reference to prior historical greatness is
crucial. Research has shown that referencing an often
threatened or lost common past both polarizes societies
and constitutes the recipe for modern tribalism. The
narrative of an identity under threat is thus the very
foundation of most autocratic regimes centered on
a "strong leader" with a cynical personal interest in
stoking hatred and antagonism to maintain his power
base. As the American scholars Steven Levitsky and
Daniel Ziblatt have addressed in their book *How
Democracies Die*, the modern death of democracies
rarely materializes at a coup or a tyrannical seizure
of power. Rather, the strategy often involves a polling
station to at least make the exercise look like "real"
democracy.

What are the flashpoints for tribalism today?
Tribalism, or neo-nationalism, is apparent from one
end of Europe to the other. In Catalonia, for instance,
where secessionists claim to urgently need a separate
Catalan state, despite having one of the highest degrees
of regional autonomy in Europe. Or in Britain, where
tribalism for more than three years has resonated
in Brexiteers' call to defy Europe in the name of
a long-expired glorious past. Similar developments
are evident in Central and Eastern Europe – and
more recently Italy, where Matteo Salvini's Lega party
employs identity politics, inventing new enemies, while
at the same time blaming Europe for everything that is
deplorable. Today, however, tribalization is reappearing
everywhere and identity politics is used offensively to
create a sense of community that "others" can never
become a part of.

Precisely because these identity-political projects need attention to flourish, well-orchestrated drama and divisiveness are frequently staged as media stunts, with a conflict-obsessed press happy to serve as backup chorus. On many occasions, hype and tribal aggression are a mere cover-up, a distraction from underlying corruption and power grabbing among populistic leaders. This is plain to see among the political elite and establishment in Hungary and the Cezch Republic, for instance, where aunts, uncles, sons-in-law, and old friends of Viktor Orbán and Andrej Babiš have become wealthy by greedy scams with EU funds.[6] Meanwhile Orbán, to divert the attention of the blatant kleptocracy, stages noise in the public sphere about non-existing migrants who will soon invade the country and transform Hungary into a multiethnic doomsday scenario. By simultaneously undermining the free press and preventing the public prosecutor from investigating these transactions, Orbán avoids any accountability for his actions. Corruption has also been thriving among the separatists in Catalonia, but has been blotted out with as much solid media coverage of pro-independence and anti-Spanish troubles in the streets as possible.[7]

Apparently, the strategy is to keep the focus of the population elsewhere and silence critical media, so that the more or less corrupted elites can make their dubious transactions in peace. However, tribalization is not reserved for autocrats who need to blur their activities. Tribalist rhetoric is rearing its head in the old, well-established democracies as well. In a desperate attempt to regain support from lost voters, the political mainstream relies on tribalistic gesture politics exemplified in everything from intensified border control to laws prohibiting burkas and taking away refugees' jewelry, as has been legislated on in Denmark.[8] It also relies upon the belief that identity politics is the only strategy left "in town" when trying to hijack voters at national elections in a global, European time. For example, a recent study found that in many Western democracies, rival political blocs agree and vote together on the large majority of issues in parliament, making identity politics and harsh rhetoric against foreigners (and the EU) the only thing left to catch voters' attention. Of course, this does not mean that identity issues cannot be significant; for example, problems of the integration of immigrants (which is often the locus) can be very real. Of course such problems have to be addressed. The point here is merely that in many contexts, identity (posturing as *real* problems) has become *the* central focal point of modern politics – even in those parts of Europe that on the surface appear more peaceful.

The question is now: how will all this affect the future of Europe? What consequences will tribalization have for the Union's survival? I will try to answer these questions by looking at three cases that, in my view, are emblematic of the tribal tendencies overtaking Europe in these years. Each is different and has its different features, but all are symptomatic of the present epoch of disintegration. The Catalan independence campaign, the anti-European Brexit crusade, and the animosity-ridden democratic backsliding in Central and Eastern Europe epitomize Europe in the year 2020. In the pages that follow, I will try to unravel the dynamics behind the smokescreen, and even more, our strange unwillingness to forcefully counteract it.

Introduction

My overall argument is that after Trump, Brexit, and the rise of populism in numerous European countries, we face a fundamental lack of confidence in the values and institutions we have built since the Second World War. Rather than insisting on our common principles and ideals, many erstwhile defenders of the liberal world order have become apologetic and therefore complicit cheerleaders for tribalism. To understand the severity of the transformations we are witnessing, we need to reconsider how the shift toward identity politics has also influenced our way of understanding democracy. In the book's second half, I argue that both populism and tribalism have helped undermine our former awareness that democracy is *more* than just elections, referenda, and parliamentary majorities. In the age of populism, where the "the people" have taken center stage, democracy seems to have atrophied to just that: majorities (also in referenda) without the rule of law, absent an open and critical exchange of views. One today rarely gets sympathy for insisting that independent counter-majoritarian institutions like courts (sometimes even supranational!) should be strengthened to uphold basic principles. Attacking counter-majoritarian bodies as well as law beyond the state has become part of the tribal spirit.

Democracy in the age of populism has thus become unconstrained majority rule, with political debate reduced to fake news and cultural fundamentalism. Equating democracy with an extreme version of majoritarianism, in which the rule of law and judicial institutions (inside as well as outside the state border) are readily questioned and even sometimes dismantled, is an extremely dangerous path to go down. And when this is wedded to crude campaigning centered on identity politics, with greater stress placed on getting the message across than on it being true, then the original meaning of liberal democracy is long lost.

In contemporary Europe, leaders also seem hesitant to insist that the European Union must embrace fundamental democratic values and ideals and make these the focal point of the community. Or rather: they insist on it in their speeches, treaties, and laws, but when push comes to shove, when it truly counts and action is needed, the courage vanishes. And yet our values need defending, now more than ever. In a world where we as Europeans are surrounded by non-democracies and regimes that fundamentally question and suppress the ideals of the Enlightenment, there can and should be no cherry-picking – no compromise when it comes to standing up for our values and ideals. We must insist on all those aspects of democracy that secure our right to speak up against the government, to hold free and fair elections, to host free universities and a free press. If we do not insist on this and if European leaders cease backing this up, in my opinion, the EU has signed its own death warrant. What is Europe meant to defend, at home and abroad, if not these values? If we fail to go on the offensive and actively oppose the tribalist forces we currently face, democracy in its true conception may soon become a thing of the past.

Imagined Communities
and Identity Politics

"We have made Italy. Now we must make Italians."
This now famous statement appears in the unfinished
memoirs of Italian statesman and writer Massimo
d'Azeglio (1798–1866). He played a fundamental role
in the unification of the Italian peninsula – a process
that was officially completed in 1870. By stressing that
the creation of a unified state with formal authority
was only the first step, d'Azeglio was conceding that
the most difficult part remained to come: the creation
of an Italian people – and of a common identity. What
provoked many later nationalists (and scholars) was
d'Azeglio's claim that identity isn't "just there" to be
dug up from the ground, but must be created – often by
elites, and often from above.

The British historian and political scientist Benedict
Anderson[1] picked up on d'Azeglio's points in an important
work of his own, *Imagined Communities: Reflections on
the Origin and Spread of Nationalism*. Here Anderson

systematically demonstrates the so-called "thesis of modernity," which points to how national identities and history are products of narratives that only gain meaning as remembrance, and thus a sense of unity, when used in stories and encounters from one generation to the next. Communities and their corresponding identities have always been "imagined" and created by people. They are not "naturally given" in the sense that they have always been there, as the so-called primordialists would otherwise claim. As the Danish historian Uffe Østergaard puts it, the thesis of modernity has never been repudiated by historians: "the thesis of modernity, that nations and national identities are largely the result of relatively few intellectuals' conscious efforts to 'construct' or 'invent' these, only becomes real later when a great majority starts acting as if the identities were 'real.'"[2]

In Europe in the eighteenth and nineteenth centuries, *national* identities were created and nurtured by elites, often with an explicit personal interest in shaping a given community's common mores, identity, and conceptions.

Anderson sees the rise of print technology, Christianity, and the educational system in particular as essential to the creation of "deep horizontal comradeship" in the nation-building process in Europe. More importantly, though identities were socially constructed, they were experienced as genuine. Only in this way could identities be meaningful, powerful, and mobilizing.

In line with Anderson and the many historians and political scientists he inspired, it is now widely recognized that all our divergent national identities have been shaped and cultivated through the school system as an unambiguous nation-building exercise.

The nation-state was a product of the French Revolution and the Napoleonic Wars, and thus a European invention. It was only after the Second World War that the idea of the nation-state "went global" and became the common organizing mode for the world. The difference between the European *territorial* states and the *nation*-state was precisely the formation of identity itself, which proved to be far stronger and more enduring than most had expected. In the nineteenth century in many cases, the initial goal was to use identity as a mobilizing force to convince young men to go to war for a higher purpose.[3] As families had to sacrifice their sons freely, rulers knew that they would only do so obediently if presented with an idea that transcended their earthly being – the nation. Joseph Weiler puts this well: "The (national) collective transcends the life of any individual – and automatically bestows, on each and every one to whom it belongs, both a past and a future."[4]

It is important to reiterate here that simply because most historical pasts and presents are manmade creations, they are not, for this reason, less real. Identities are very real to those who live them, who believe in them, and whose leaders marshal them in the fight against opposing rivals. My point is not to state this rather obvious fact. Rather it is to emphasize that the cultivation of an *exclusive identity*, and the possible use of it as a weapon against others, is not at all an innocent exercise. One cannot simply dig up and adopt mores from the past or long-lost historical linkages of the kind today's populists and their tribal cousins take on as signs of identity. These are not constituent elements of personalities and nations, but traits that are shaped and cultivated.

When this is done strategically, we are far away from the idea of the nation as a home for merely peaceful co-existence. However, today we tend to forget that most European (and other) nation-states are exactly that: products of war, ethnic cleansing, flight, and expulsions. When used in modern politics in these years, we may call the phenomenon "fabricated tribalism." Fabricated tribalism is part of a cynical power game in which political leaders exploit a feeling of belonging to mobilize against well-defined enemies. Amy Chua has described how tribalism has become a central new part of world politics today:

> tribalism remains a powerful force everywhere; indeed, in recent years, it has begun to tear at the fabric of liberal democracies in the developed world, and even the postwar liberal international order. To truly understand today's world and where it is heading, one must acknowledge the power of tribalism. Failing to do so will only make it stronger.[5]

"Fabricated" tribalism, where culture and identity are employed deliberately for political mobilization, can also be seen as a form of activist identity policy. Identity politics are proliferating everywhere today – not only in Europe. Most people recognize the discussion of identity politics from America, where left-leaning minority groups are accused of being too concerned with their own specific grievances to face issues of broader concern for society. In this book, identity politics is first and foremost seen as a national or (in the case of Catalonia) regional project. What the two have in common is the dangerous tendency to put identity or culture *before* politics. Why is this immensely problematic? Because while *political* projects and arguments can be debated and questioned, *culture* and *identity* belong to a different sphere that is largely impervious to critical engagement. I will come back to this point further on, but it is essential to note here that shifting a project from the political to the identitarian or cultural sphere removes it from ordinary political contestation and places it in a privileged realm where it purports to be immune to counterclaims. A political movement or proposal is always up for debate, but being based on emotions and beliefs (rather than facts), cultural or identarian projects are inevitably beyond discussion.

Tribal and identitarian discourse spans the political spectrum. Some have called populism and nationalism "the identity politics of the right."[6] Then there are hybrid cases, such as secessionism in Catalonia, in which soi-disant progressives often employ the same kind of exclusionary rhetoric favored by right-wing nationalists.

In both cases, when political campaigners use identity to boost their popularity and power, fear, scaremongering, and "us/them rhetoric" are essential ingredients. The purpose may be nationalist or separatist, but the techniques employed are the same. At the same time, it is necessary to deny this is happening. The legitimacy and power of these movements depend entirely on their authenticity.

Contemporary tribalist movements have worked to keep up appearances, claiming to have a substantive and important project while denying their identitarian curse on Spanish unionists, EU elites, or "cosmopolitan liberals" – though Orbán admitted quite openly that he has declared war on Muslim migrants. Identity politics even came into play when Donald Trump cleverly mobilized against "the Washington swamp" in 2016. Creating and sustaining the conflict is crucial to the tribalistic project, but it is at the same time important that it doesn't look too identitarian to work. We saw it when Brexit campaigners talked about their opponents, the Remainers, as unpatriotic traitors seduced by European federal ideals.[7] In their eyes, the European idea is a stab in the back of true Britishness, which would fare much better on its own.

The same emphasis on betrayal has also been utilized strategically by the secessionist movement in Catalonia. Again and again, the discourse of treason and betrayal crops up in characterizations of Catalan unionists' (who constitute a majority) opposition to independence.

Identity politics and its accompanying tribalist rhetoric make fewer cognitive demands than calls for increased unity and collaboration. It appeals to the stomach, often to blood, history, and territory, rather than asking people to conceive of ways to bridge cultural differences. As Timothy Garton Ash writes:

> [T]he populists tell a simplistic story about how pulling up the national drawbridge and 'taking back control' will result in the restoration of an imagined golden past of good jobs, happy families and a more traditional national community.[8]

Though Ash is referring specifically to Brexit campaigners here, the script is the same for the other identitarian projects we discuss in this book. All that is required is slight adjustments to fit the circumstances.

Modern identitarian campaigning has also become much more professionalized. These days, little is left to chance when it comes to luring voters and supporters. Campaigns rely on well-designed storylines produced in corporate headquarters by highly paid spin doctors and professional strategists educated at the best universities. Excluding here professional trolls and the use of algorithms to sway people's minds, the psychology behind what one might term "modern engineered tribalism" has turned into a "neurological big business," as Chua describes tellingly in her recent book *Political Tribes*. Chua discusses the "dark side of the tribal instinct," with strategists and strongmen developing campaigns designed to play on "group-bonding" fear and on the "dehumanizing" of their opponents.[9]

This is probably why tribalists often refer to their critics and opponents as traitors.[10] Treason and betrayal are strong words, and their repeated employment shows how identitarian references are often carefully designed to obtain specific political objectives. Critique and satire become dangerous because they reveal the absence of a proper essence in these projects, and in this way resemble the Franciscan church's attempt to suppress laughter and irony in Umberto Eco's 1980 novel *The Name of the Rose*. Irony establishes a critical distance, and to the extent that it grades into ridicule, it is dangerous and must be stamped out, whatever the cost. Few tribalists have been able to tolerate ridicule or satire, as we see in authoritarian leaders' continuous attempts to ban critical media and satiric cartoonists. As when the Chinese leader Xi Jinping seemingly banned Winnie-the-Pooh because an American talk show host made fun of Xi by comparing the two.

Identity as an instrument of mobilization against the enemy has existed in many different settings over centuries – above all in war. And yet there is little discussion of the belligerent tone of identitarian figures from secessionists to Brexiteers. When Brexiteers argue that the UK is too culturally and historically distinct from the rest of Europe to be a mere subject of a European Union.[11] Or when they argue (as Boris Johnson has done on several occasions) that the UK would have been reduced to a vassal state if the "surrender bill" of Theresa May – Johnson's predecessor – had ever been adopted. Secessionists in Catalonia equally make these kinds of allegations. For instance, when they claim that the Catalans' language, history, and culture are so specific – and so frequently suppressed – that they require not only their own state, but also – in the interim – the near-eradication of the Spanish language from the Catalan schooling system.[12] As Nacho Martín Blanco, a member of the Catalan parliament, has put it: "Catalonia has the dubious honor of being the only place in the Western world where the majority of the population do not even have the option of enrolling their children in schools that teach in their native language."[13] Even in the Basque Country, another of Spain's troubled regions, things have not gone this far.

Replacing politics with identity or culture is an extremely potent but also explosive weapon. Potent because, by putting identity and ethnic/cultural belonging above all, it posits the existence of a deeper, more innocent, purer stratum *beyond the political*. And dangerous because its proponents refuse to acknowledge the political nature of their positions, which naturally would make them an object of discussion.

The tribalism and ethnocentrism we face cannot, however, be reduced to secessionist movements or radical Tories' views of the EU–UK relationship. It is far more wide-ranging than that.

Tribal rhetoric and identity politics are systematically employed by illiberal demagogues like Viktor Orbán, who touts Hungary's cultural uniqueness while attacking foreigners, Jews, LBGTQ activists, and anything that reeks of cosmopolitanism. He presents the liberal elite as the enemy – reckless globalists imposing multicultural values and tolerance on innocent nativist Hungarians.

Orbán presents the nation's distinctiveness – reinforced with Christianity, to get the older generation on board – as something precious to be shielded from an invasive disease. Hungarian society was full of hope thirty years ago, when it broke free from the Soviet yoke. Under Orbán, it has not only embraced identity politics full force, but even turned its back on the core values of democracy.

The purpose of the identitarian projects I have so far described is to transform identity from a passive, historical sentiment to an active weapon against more inclusive forms of nationhood (such as Spanish unity), Europeanization, or globalization. With Europe's current immigration debacle, which has called the otherwise successful Schengen open-border regime into question, new walls and fences are again being built and campaigned for.

Tribal Thinking and Dreams of Detachment

Catalonia is one of the places in Europe where issues of tribal rhetoric and renewed borders have been most prominent in recent years. On October 1, 2017, the Catalan regional government held an illegal referendum on independence from Spain. A few days later the independence movement's leader, Carles Puigdemont, declared the establishment of a new Catalan state. Though the referendum was recognized neither in Spain nor abroad, it shined a light on a deeply divided region that has paralyzed Spanish society in many ways for years, if not decades. Long-simmering anger and resentment, going back to the Franco regime, in which Catalans were unable to speak their language or cultivate their identity, have turned nearly upside down today. Now the unionists – paradoxically, the numerical majority – are intimidated and prevented from airing their opinions publicly. Catalan separatists control the educational institutions, the police, cultural and environmental institutions, transportation, and commerce, and completely dominate public broadcasting. In November

2019 things escalated, as 800 university professors[1] from Catalan universities complained in an open letter about years of censorship and intimidation from a separatist, loyal university management. What made things explode was that the university leaders so openly sided with the Catalan separatist politicians who were given severe prison sentences after a year-long trial for having encouraged and enabled the illegal vote for independence in October 2017. The Catalan university leaders thus encouraged the professors to cancel teaching and exams in protest, while they stood quietly by as hooded activists blocked the classrooms.

Catalan language policy in particular – now predominant in all public schools and universities – has been decisive for the separatists, enabling them to cultivate support for independence among the youth. Benedict Anderson has cogently laid out the importance of language for identity-production. Language is central because it generates the ground for "a new form of imagined community which in its basic morphology sets the stage for the modern state."[2] The emphasis on language as a form of national self-consciousness goes back to the German philosophers Johann Gottlieb Fichte and Johann Gottfried Herder, but likely achieved its most potent expression with the historian Elie Kedourie, who stressed the role of language for independence movements in general.[3]

Though there has been far-reaching debate about Catalan linguistic policies, few Spanish governments have dared to enforce the Constitutional Court's verdict from 2000, which declared Spanish "the working language" – even in Catalonia. One reason may be that the court failed to define specifically what this entails.[4]

Although Spanish today – as mentioned previously – is reduced to the same hours of teaching as English in the schools and most Catalonians speak both Catalan and Spanish brilliantly, the reduction of Spanish to a secondary language is obviously a demonstration of power and identity politics full force.

The present-day independence surge in Catalonia is a conflict that affects everyone and splits society, families, and friends down the middle. From an outsider's perspective however, the 2017 referendum comes across as a disorganized public relations stunt. Many observers noted that it fell short of even the most basic democratic principles and rules (which was probably intentional). There were no measures to prevent duplicate voting and no official institution monitoring the proceedings to assure that the process followed international standards. Even harder to take seriously was Carles Puidgemont's state formation, which claimed the support of 90 percent of Catalans, though it is known that only a minority – 43 percent – bothered to cast their vote.[5] And yet, from a PR perspective, the chaos and buzz that followed contributed seamlessly to the international attention Puigdemont had hoped to achieve.

* * *

Let us take a closer look at the Catalan identity movement with a reality check from the European perspective. Catalan separatists claim – like the Scots who voted on independence from Great Britain in 2014 – that they want to join, or rather "stay" in, the EU when they leave their mother nation. The possibility of fast-tracking the normal admission procedures has thus been taken for granted by most secessionists.[6]

And yet there is nothing to suggest that the EU would admit Catalonia through a kind of fast-track procedure if it were to achieve independence from Spain.[7] As expert in international law Cristina Fasone has recently pointed out: "Article 4(2) clarifies that national identity (singular) comprises the fundamental structures, political and constitutional, inclusive of regional and local self-government. It follows that regional and local self-government, being part of national identity, is not something for the EU to take into consideration and to regulate."[8] Despite what the Catalan separatists' leaders have promised their followers, the EU has, in other words, been very reluctant even to comment on any of the ongoing secessionist disputes – the one in Catalonia as well as the Scottish equivalent.

This reluctance on the part of the EU is not only comprehensible, but also wise. First of all – and most importantly for my argument here – the EU is by definition a multi-state entity and a universalistic project striving both for unity and for the protection of diversity, as the motto has it in various official EU documents. In this sense separatism is – and always will be – antithetical to European ideals. It will never become EU policy to encourage identity politics as exercised by the independence movement in Catalonia. Antagonism and animosity among regional and state cultures never were and never will be what Europe is about.

Joseph Weiler uses even stronger words:

"Europe should not appear as a Nirvana for that form of irredentist Euro-tribalism which contradicts the deep values and needs, not only of the Union as a political institution, but of Europe's noble attempt to move away from its sanguinary past."[9]

And as he continues: It would be hugely ironic ... if the prospect of membership in the European Union ended up providing an incentive for an ethos of political disintegration."

Even if separatists had no intention of undermining the European project, spreading disintegration and fragmentation could easily be an unintended consequence. In other words: rewarding secession with EU membership is unlikely to be the route the EU takes.

There is also another, more straightforward reason why the EU stays far, far away from supporting the internal splitting up of democratic member states, and that relates to power politics on a very basic level: the plain fact that member states alone enjoy the status of formal, legal constituents of the Union. The heads of state and government are unlikely to do away with this status and its related power any time soon. Would the EU never interfere, then? Certainly, it would in the event of an outright military coup, the suppression of local minorities, or a serious breach of the rule of law – as observed in Poland and Hungary. In general, as long as a member state confronts its internal problems through its own democratic institutions, as has been the case in Spain, the EU will not – and should not – interfere. But as we shall see in the case for Hungary and Poland (and one could add several others), where the rule of law is so blatantly threatened, the EU (or at least some parts of the EU) currently works to counter policies detrimental to European and democratic values.[10]

A second reason why the EU has been extremely hesitant to engage in the ongoing dispute between Catalonia and Madrid is that doing so could inspire other Spanish regions and stir up unrest among European secessionists elsewhere aspiring to similar attention. Finally, there is a legitimate fear in the EU that intervention might severely undermine European unity and cohesion. It is important to emphasize that this in no way means that the EU leadership supported the Rajoy government's severe and clumsy handling of the Catalan referendum. For most outside observers, it was painfully apparent that the crisis was dealt with ineptly. Behind the scenes in the EU, then Prime Minister Rajoy was undoubtedly encouraged to enter into dialogue with separatist leaders and resolve the Catalan issue in a nonviolent and less confrontational manner. Spain's current Prime Minister, Pedro Sánchez, seems to wish to proceed in this direction. However, despite the fact that he won the parliamentary elections in November 2019, the problem is obviously not resolved. The discrepancies will undoubtably continue – also in light of the conviction of the Catalan politicians in October 2019. The new style and approach that Sánchez has laid out are, however, important. Rajoy believed that the separatists could be intimidated by using force and otherwise stayed quiet when the secessionists used their enormous propaganda machinery, especially in foreign media. This was not a wise strategy. As we have seen in the Brexit campaign in the UK, if you do not attack fake news and blatant lies head on, it is these and not the truth that will survive.

Having said this, we should keep in mind that during the early stages, the EU encouraged and perhaps even fueled dis-integrative policies for regions in pursuit of broader assimilation. Multiple sources suggest the EU initially wished to use regions as a tool to soften and even bypass the resistance of occasionally intransigent

member states. An example of this was its recognition early on of languages like Catalan and Welsh
as co-official languages.[11] Also the establishment of
the Committee of the Regions sent some "conflicting
signals" that might not have been approved by member
states (or the EU itself) today.[12]

The earlier focus on regions may also appear slightly
contradictory and unnecessary today, considering
developments over the past fifteen to twenty years in the
EU. In this period member states have become more and
more central, from the establishment of the European
Council in 1974 to that of a permanent President of the
European Council in 2009.[13] Both reconfirm that the
member states remain the constituent parts of the EU
and that the regions continue to play a marginal role.

However, it is not the case that the EU has abstained
entirely from engaging in the debate on detachment.
The Commission, as the EU's executive arm, has previously strongly warned against it. The former head of
the European Commission, Manuel Barroso, made
this unmistakably clear in relation to the Scottish
independence vote in 2014, stating that any new
independent entity seceding from a member state would
only be able to reenter the EU under Article 49 TEU.[14] In
practical terms, this means that any region or territory
that achieves independence from an EU member state
will inevitably be regarded as a third country and have
to (re)apply to the EU in accordance with the ordinary
accession procedures.

While from an international law perspective, the
unilateral decision to secede is not a legal right,[15] experts
have pointed out that circumstances matter. Much will
depend on the way any concrete act of secession is

undertaken and the history behind it. If an attempt at independence is considered constitutional and legitimate from the perspective of the member state involved, political realities and the EU might be more accommodating.

The Scottish independence referendum in 2014 is in fact a good example of this. Because it was organized in accordance with legal procedure, with the support of the British government and parliament, and in compliance with the EU's fundamental values, Scotland's wish to separate from the UK might have merited a more pragmatic approach than the Catalan wish. Brexit may moreover be a factor in any future Scottish vote on independence, and the Scottish Brexit frustrations are directly and indirectly being acknowledged in the EU. Scotland being a region extremely supportive of Europe (in the Brexit referendum, 62 percent voted to remain in the EU) might incline the EU further toward possible Scottish membership. This is only speculation, however. A possible negative factor for Scotland's EU prospects is that the hostile (and unlawful) Catalonian secession attempt will have preceded it. However, it is interesting that Josep Borell, Spain's former socialist Foreign Minister and now the EU's foreign policy chief, stated in an interview that if a new referendum on Scottish independence reemerges and takes place according to democratic principles, and Brexit is a reality, he cannot see a problem in a fast-paced EU membership for Scotland. This statement aroused some attention, as Borell, himself a Catalan, has combatted Catalan independence fiercely. In his usual blatant style, Borell also stated that he was far more concerned for the breakup of Britain, as a result of Brexit, than this happening to Spain.

———

We must acknowledge here that law and politics are two different things. Therefore, it is difficult to predict in advance how the EU would respond to an independent Scotland. However, we do know that Scottish leader Nicola Sturgeon has already announced that – when Brexit becomes a reality – she will seek a new vote for Scottish independence as early as 2020!

If we overlook the breakup of totalitarian empires like the Soviet Union, which resulted in fifteen new states (many of which stayed highly totalitarian), secessionism still constitutes what I define as a "tribal shift." Nationalist projects that seek to replace a broader, more inclusive democratic identity with a narrower identitarian project remain, generally speaking, a step backward. Moreover, one wonders where the lines should be drawn? For instance, as Catalan separatists are mainly located in the countryside while the unionists constitute a large majority in Barcelona, should the logic of the tribe then not permit the city to break free as well?

This may seem like an ironic provocative question, but it is in fact a principled and important one.

Weiler is particularly harsh on the subject of an – in principle – ethnically "cleansed" Catalonia and its prospects for entering the EU after a break from Spain. As he puts it with – in my view – extraordinary acuity:

> Why would there be an interest in accepting into the Union a polity such as an independent Catalonia predicated on such a regressive and outmoded nationalist ethos which apparently cannot stomach the discipline of loyalty and solidarity which one would expect it would owe to its fellow citizens in Spain?[16]

Catalonia has disqualified itself from ever becoming a Union member on pure moral grounds, argues Weiler:

> the very demand for independence from Spain, an independence from the need to work out political, social, cultural and economic differences within the Spanish polity, independence from the need to work through and transcend history, arguably morally and politically disqualify Catalonia, and the like, as future Member States of the European Union.

We will return to the question of Catalonia when discussing the increasing use of referenda and the changing conceptions of democracy in a time of populism. Populists thus frequently promote referenda as more democratic and legitimate than ordinary representative democracy. Puigdemont stressed this point, as he and his sympathizers in October 2017 used this particular instrument in their fight against Madrid. Below I oppose this notion and argue that democracy is – and must be – about more than posing yes/no questions whose outcome is uncertain to all.

Putting this aside, we have yet to even examine the practical issues entailed by an EU composed of dozens of small tribal states. Imagine EU decision-making structures overtaken by a cluster of small, even ethnically "clean," introverted statelets with nationalist ideologies and sealed borders. We are, in many ways, already part-way there, as several member states for years now have closed off their frontiers in violation of the Schengen principles. And enabling the EU to speak with a single voice on the world stage is already difficult with twenty-eight – or now twenty-seven – member states. Attempting it with fifty or more ethnic enclaves would be a disaster, and a deathblow to Europe as we know it.

Why Brexit is Just Another Kind of Tribalism

Brexit is in many ways just a different form of secessionism – where the object of its animadversion is the EU. Accompanying the culturally identitarian and political crusade against the European community, Brexit represents another common tribal current: a genuine repugnance for being legally bound by any institution or regime beyond the state. Hostility toward multilateral (or, in the case of the EU, supranational) cooperation is a common feature of many populist movements challenging the international order in these years.

It is thus difficult to see Brexit as something other than an abandonment of the universal values the European project represents. It fundamentally questions the virtues of the pooling of sovereignty logic that was the foundation of the entire liberal order after the Second World War. There is therefore little doubt that the British decision to leave the EU was regarded – at least at first – as a threat to this order and to the EU itself.

It would take a psychiatrist and countless therapy sessions to decipher the true root causes of Brexit, which has taken years of internal quarrel to become a reality. My focus here will therefore be on the identitarian dimension together with the closely related sovereignty issue that has marked Britain for ages but has become increasingly obvious. There is little doubt that the obsession with parliamentary sovereignty and the concurrent suspicion toward international courts and supranational institutions feed into the general populist onslaught against European law and institutions – which former British Foreign Minister Jeremy Hunt compared to the Soviet Union.[1]

When the Brits first announced that they had voted to leave the European Union on June 23, 2016, the European public was paralyzed. Historian and columnist Anne Appelbaum suggested, in a now famous column in the *Washington Post* in March 2016, that Brexit – along with Trump in the White House and Marine Le Pen in the Élysée Palace in Paris – could spell the end of the West as we know it.[2] In the first months after the British referendum, most observers were in shock, not least at the anger that apparently was hidden in the soul of the British people. How could so many have been so wrong about the feelings of ordinary Brits? Where did the uprising come from and what would be the consequences? This was eagerly debated among opinion makers and commentators, the vast majority of whom never foresaw that a country like Britain would opt out of the EU. The debate was for the most part focused on the possible domino effects triggered by Brexit, but there also was a massive focus on the faults and shortcomings of the EU. Many thus predicted similar uprisings in other EU countries. Maybe because they were baffled by how poorly they had been able to predict the sentiments of the crowds. Little by little a new narrative developed: the so-called "globalists" had overruled and neglected ordinary people. Even among those who did not immediately buy this new narrative, there was considerable concern.

After the Brexit vote, there was understandably a fear that the European project would lose its legitimacy also with the European public. Therefore, the media was dominated by doomsday prophecies, and the perspective of the EU's impending doom also became trendy among researchers. Maybe European unity was just a bracket in world history? The multiple national elections in the spring of 2017 became "the big test" of whether Europeans as such had turned their back on the EU (and thus the elites), voting into office instead the many new populist leaders who had surged not only in the shadow of Brexit but also after the election of Donald Trump. However, this thesis was quickly rebuffed as it was realized that Brexit probably mainly had to do with the "English" loss of imperial identity (and fifteen years of conservative austerity) rather than with anything going on on the continent. In Austria, in the Netherlands, and in France – where Macron to the great relief of many won the presidential elections convincingly – populism (in France, personified by Marine Le Pen) was sent out into the cold.

There is, however, no doubt that the complete inability of the British leaders, Theresa May and Boris Johnson, to handle Brexit in anything resembling a well-ordered manner was surprising for most. After following the meltdown of British domestic (and EU) politics and negotiations for three years, most observers on the continent simply concluded that the more than

300-year-old British democracy had become completely dysfunctional. Moreover, where Brexit initially was thought to be the beginning of the end of the EU, it now seems that Brexit is the single event in the history of the EU that has had the largest effect in turning EU skeptics into firm supporters. Brexit has thus been a wake-up call, not only for the heads of state and government, but also among ordinary people, who with disbelief have witnessed the utter collapse of British domestic politics. As the former Head of the European Council, Donald Tusk, put it, "Brexit had become a vaccination instead of a virus." Rather than being seen as a threat to the EU, Brexit may thus turn out to become a regrettable but potentially first step toward broader popular support for European unity.

Under the leadership of former minister and Commissioner Michel Barnier, the EU has shown surprising resolve in its reaction to Britain's decision. The UK on the other hand has yet to make clear, even three years after voting to leave, what kind of future arrangement it is looking for post-Brexit.[3] At the time of writing, the British government still has no vision for the future EU–UK relationship, which will have to be negotiated and eventually turned into a formal trade deal – something which normally takes years rather than months. Despite Boris Johnson's new Brexit deal, it is thus still uncertain whether the UK will end up remaining, perhaps for decades, in a kind of EEA arrangement, copying EU legislation but having no say as to its contents.

There are, moreover, many indications that a long-term consequence of Brexit could be the breakup of the United Kingdom into old national tribes. Northern

Ireland, which is set to remain in the EU's single market, may end up reuniting with Ireland, while Scotland, which as mentioned above has already announced plans for a new referendum on independence, may well leave the UK too.

Due to the new border in the Irish Sea, "Little England" could thus in a decade become all that is left of the Great British Empire.[4] Interestingly, many of the English Brexiteers who usually long for the old empire have indicated that losing Scotland and Northern Ireland would be a price worth paying for Brexit.[5]

The hardcore Brexiteers are clearly furthest away from those who strive to keep the UK together and as connected as possible to the EU's internal market. Like many other nationalists (and even secessionists), they still consider sovereignty a zero-sum game in which each party acquires more sovereignty and more control when it isolates itself and withdraws from international commitments. The same thinking is evident in Donald Trump, who believes multilateral cooperation weakens rather than strengthens the US. And yet the question in 2020 is: what do you do with your sovereignty once you have managed to formally reclaim it? If it leaves you isolated and dependent on rules and circumstances made by others, have you then truly reclaimed your sovereignty or rather relinquished more of it by withdrawing? The answer, to my mind, is clearly the latter.

Nowadays sovereignty is *not* the zero-sum game it may have been in the past, but one where power consists in the exercise of sovereignty by influencing the rules that govern your country under all circumstances – whether inside or outside the EU. If you retreat you will lose because – no matter which arrangement you end up in – you will be dependent on rules, standards, and laws drawn up by others. To have power today in the modern world is to make and influence rules. It is not to retreat into splendid isolation. This is undoubtedly so for those wealthy nations that have the goal of remaining wealthy and continuing trading freely with the EU block. And the access to a market of more than 400 million consumers will effect the private economy of Mr. and Mrs. Smith – like it or not. The EU would, however, never accept standards different from their own strict rules on food and goods. Why accept products with lower or different environmental standards, or weaker protections for workers and residents, when this might automatically welcome unfair competition? The EU won't – and they never will, so whether the Brits end up with a Norwegian solution or a Canadian-style agreement on trade, they will have to accept European rules and standards for every product they produce if they want to sell in the European market. And so, we are back with the sovereignty question: why not stay in the club and influence the rules that will govern you? Many of us have asked this question repeatedly throughout the histrionic Brexit showdown. French President Macron did the same in his Sorbonne speech in 2017, trying to persuade Europeans to start thinking of sovereignty no longer as a property of individual European states, but as something you only sustain by exercising it in common. We should – Macron argues – not harp on and insulate individual states' sovereignty, but promote and project a European sovereignty we all share in. Instead of quarreling between ourselves, we should measure European sovereignty against global powers (the US, Russia, China, etc.) with which we as Europeans are in constant competition. And as I will argue later, not just with regard to economic and defense capabilities, but also in values.

This new conception of sovereignty has, however, not convinced the Brits so far. Though Brexit will surely turn out much worse for the UK than for the EU, the idea of a country preferring to follow its own destiny rather than staying in the European family *is* thus a symptom of the underlying tribal current that colors Europe of late. And a further splitting up of the UK would of course only confirm this. For tribalists, the building of new borders, fences, and walls is, however, considered more desirable than shared sovereignty. This may not – intentionally – mean relinquishing all European ideals and values, but putting identity first necessarily represents a step backward and contributes to the formation of a Europe in which the tribal logic increasingly reigns. As Dutch historian Koert Debeuf has argued, putting the tribal question is a much broader perspective: "in 1989, the year the Berlin Wall fell, the world had 15 walls or fences between countries. Today, this number has risen to more than 70."[6]

* * *

In the case of Brexit, tribalism is not just about identity politics in a narrow sense, denouncing Europe and looking back on past glory. It is also about fake news, scare campaigns, and a general scapegoating of international institutions, made worse by Russian meddling.

The American writer Timothy Snyder paints an ominous picture of events in his 2018 book *The Road to Unfreedom*, in which he describes the forceful return of authoritarianism and Russian influence, which spread from Russia after 2010, through Eastern Europe and into the West.[7] In Snyder's opinion, it is primarily Putin who has strategically cultivated new friends among nationalist radicals in a deliberate attempt to dissolve Western institutions. Elections in several Western countries have been affected and, according to British journalist Carole Cadwallader's elaborate and detailed documentation, the Brexit vote was affected as well, even though it is of course difficult to prove what exactly made people vote as they did at the ballot box. [8]

A different, yet related question – which we will deal with further in the second half of the book – is the wonder of the British decades-long wrangling over the European Convention on Human Rights. It is striking that not only the British but multiple Western politicians and writers on the right have begun questioning the Convention in parallel with their criticism of other binding European rules and institutions.

For years, the Russians have tried to delegitimize not only multilateral treaties and the EU itself, but also the European Convention on Human Rights and the European Court of Human Rights in Strasbourg in which they themselves take reluctantly part.[9] Interestingly, some Western politicians are now asking whether the entire existence of a supranational regime that interferes in national affairs is even a good idea, proposing that protection of rights could just as well be left to *national* courts and parliaments.

The question being raised is whether supranational institutions, with the competence to intervene and overrule national law, are fair and democratically acceptable. The attitude in countries such as Britain and

Denmark has in recent years been that the protection of rights could and *should* be left to national courts and especially the politicians of national parliaments. While, on the surface, this may seem uncontroversial, one wonders where this indirect and perhaps unintentional undermining of crucial liberal institutions, which many Western politicians often praise while blaming non-democracies for not respecting them, actually originates from.

We will deal further with this issue later, but the point here is that the undermining of the liberal world order often starts at home (if sometimes with the help of the Russians!). When politicians and opinion makers start discussing the costs and benefits of EU membership, or questioning whether human rights really are universal or should rather be determined by individual countries' own politicians, then Putin has gotten exactly what he is striving for.

One of those who have repeatedly questioned both liberal democracy and human rights commitments, contemptuously denouncing them as just "liberal" Western values, is Hungary's Viktor Orbán. His so-called "illiberalism" is the third leg of the analysis of tribalist megatrends.

The Tribal Shift in Central and Eastern Europe

The Bulgarian thinker Ivan Krastev has found it disturbing that voters in the former Communist bloc in Central and Eastern Europe are now voting for parties campaigning not only on anti-EU platforms, but even on anti-democratic ones.[1] The paradox, he argues, is that the very rights their elected leaders want to undermine fifteen years after the EU's expansion are largely the upshot of EU membership.

So despite generous EU funding and significant economic growth over the past years and an influential seat at the top table, things are now reversing. In the beginning everything went well, but in recent years several countries are experiencing a regress, at least when using democracy, the rule of law, and anti-corruption efforts as a benchmark. According to Transparency International's latest corruption index of 2019, Hungary is one of the most corrupt countries in the EU. Though Krastev sees the hailing of figures like Viktor Orbán in Hungary and Jaroslaw Kaczyński in Poland as illogical, he interestingly cites culture and opposition to Western liberal values among the main causes.[2] The cultivation of Christian conservative values – including the opposition to abortion and LGBTQ rights, especially among the rural population of many of the Central and Eastern European countries – has enabled transformations few believed possible. The rights to a free and critical press and to free universities are just some of the key rights that have been demeaned, but so has the right to organize against the regime, and there is an awareness that the courts, which ought to protect the individual, are no longer populated by impartial judges. These latter issues have been a particular problem during the ten-year Orbán rule in Hungary. However, it has also aroused outrage throughout Europe that, in particular, Eastern European (and Maltese) journalists who have assumed the task of mapping corruption, tax fraud, and abuse are being pursued, threatened, and even killed, as happened to 28-year-old Slovak journalist Ján Kuciak in 2018 and the Maltese Daphne Caruana Galizia in 2017. Both worked on stories that linked fraud and corruption to big business and powerful politicians and both cases are still unresolved. Ján Kuciak worked at the online media Aktuality.sk and focused on tax fraud among important businessmen in Slovakia (with close ties to significant politicians). His murder was quickly seen as a contract killing designed to choke the entire Union. In Hungary, critical journalists are also subject to extremely difficult working conditions, which I will return to, but Orbán's way of silencing critical writers is somewhat more subtle than the above-mentioned more brutal examples from Malta and Slovakia. In many ways, however, Orbán's method is far more effective. It is thus not about killing or imprisoning people he disagrees with; no, instead Orbán's oligarch friends have "bought up" the papers they dislike and replaced the editors and journalists with likeminded sympathizers. Their job description has then been to deliver the "right news" to the people.

As the *New York Times* uncovered in 2019 in a rather terrifying series of articles tellingly called "The Money Farmers,"[3] Hungary (and the Czech Republic) are moreover among the places in Europe where misuse of EU agricultural funds and corruption are worst. Many have simultaneously noticed how Orbán's use of tribal "us/them" rhetoric to garner national support for his anti-immigration policies grows in parallel with attempts to hide what is actually going on with the allocation of this generous funding from the EU. Few have, however, fully realized how, over the past decade, Orbán has also twisted democracy so radically that numerous experts with in-depth knowledge of Central and Eastern Europe today refuse to go on defining Hungary as a true democracy.

The big question is of course why voters go on supporting leaders who undermine democracy, the rule of law, and their own hard-won rights. An explanation I am inclined to believe in is exactly these leaders' skilled use of tribalist rhetoric, which reserves much of its animus for migrants to distract attention from the more fundamental dismantling of democracy. In political science this is referred to as democratic backsliding.[4] Most frightening, perhaps, is the way observers and European colleagues have failed to notice these changes over the course of the last decade.

Amid a puzzling silence from European leaders, the challenge to European rules, values, and minority rights is gaining ground in some Eastern European countries. A survey of 56,000 adults by the Pew Research Center recently confirmed that despite rising growth levels after the inclusion of Eastern and Central Europe in the EU, attitudes on values still differ markedly between East and West.[5] This is particularly true when it comes to the rights of homosexuals, the need for protecting minorities, democracy, and the value of national identities. National culture must be protected, this survey says, and thus easily becomes a weapon that can be employed in internal national self-affirmation, as well as in the fight against the liberal West, which is considered a threat to the nation and conservative family values.

What we have been witnessing in recent years in Hungary is far more alarming than most analysts, heads of state, and governments want to admit. Remember: this is a country that willingly signed up for strong liberal rules and values – the Union's Charter of Fundamental Rights and the Copenhagen criteria – when joining the EU in 2004. However, over the past ten years the Orbán regime has, quietly and without much notice, curbed most independent liberal institutions while maintaining a sense of normality by, for instance, regularly having elections. As we shall see below, however, these are by no means ordinary elections in which all positions can be expressed. Instead, the Hungarian leader has made it difficult for his competitors to access the media and thus compete on equal terms, while he has simultaneously curbed critical journalism and forced universities and NGOs out of the country. In this way he has managed to cement government power over society at large. The transformations are tremendous and perhaps even irreversible.

Let us remind ourselves of what the Copenhagen criteria consist of. The accession criteria for admitting new EU members were written in Copenhagen in 1993 at a European Council meeting. They are the essential conditions all candidate countries must abide by to become members of the EU:

- political criteria: stability of institutions guaranteeing democracy, the rule of law, human rights, and respect for and protection of minorities;
- economic criteria: a functioning market economy and the capacity to cope with competition and market forces;
- administrative and institutional capacity to effectively implement the *acquis* [that is, the EU's cumulated laws and treaties] and ability to take on the obligations of membership.[6]

These are obviously not the only criteria that members of the EU have to abide by. The Charter, the Convention of Human Rights, and the acquis Communautaire are loaded with democratic rules and norms that have to be observed by all in the club. The problem is, however, that though all these rules are clear and – for most people – almost self-evident, the EU has very few mechanisms to sanction and investigate eventual breaches. So, while the EU has excelled at enforcing its conditions prior to allowing new member states in, it has virtually no remedies in place to cope with the kind of massive democratic backlash we have seen in parts of Central and Eastern Europe in recent years.

It was hard to predict that Viktor Orbán would wind up an ardent anti-liberal. He was once a student rebel leader, fighting Communism during the revolutions

---

against Communist rule in the 1990s.[7] He even accepted a George Soros scholarship to attend Oxford University, but quickly returned. In 1998, he became Europe's youngest Prime Minister, but only years later, in 2010, did he begin winning elections for his Fidesz party on the populist, illiberal platform he now embraces. As Paul Lendvai eloquently explains in his 2018 biography of Orbán, he started off as a mainstream politician and friend of the West but has evolved into an autocratic headache for the EU. And yet, despite several critical reports from the Venice Commission, NGOs, and the European Commission itself, European leaders have largely ignored Orbán's illiberal dynasty, instead turning their – still rather weak – attention to far larger Poland, where democracy is also under stress. The current Polish government and its party PiS have copied Hungarian techniques, even expressing open admiration for Orbán's curtailment of the country's justice system – which has led to several cases before the European Court of Justice, including an infringement case for the breach of Article 2 TEU.

Thus, through a judicial reform, the Poles suddenly adjudicated that the judges of the Polish Supreme Court should retire at a younger age than previously. The consequence of this was that approximately a third of the judges could be removed by the government and new, more government-friendly judges could be deployed. The threat of sacking (or early retirement of) the judges obviously questioned the entire foundation of the rule of law in Poland. So did the addition made by the Poles that if a judge wanted to stay longer, he or she should apply for permission from the country's President – a President appointed by the government and a long-time member of PiS. A similar maneuver took place in Hungary in 2011. Here the European Court of Justice ruled that Hungary had violated the independence of the judiciary by forcing judges to retire. Orbán accepted the verdict – apparently at least; however, the "old" judges, who had been dismissed, had already been replaced by new, younger, government-friendly judges when the European Court's verdict was finally delivered.

One of the few heads of state and government who has openly and loudly warned of the backlash against democracy in Europe is French President Emmanuel Macron. For him, the 2019 European elections became a direct test of liberal democracy, calling for serious opposition to illiberalism. Not least because the EU, as he sees it, is more than a purely economic community, the protecting of common values is primary as well.

If we examine the result of the European Parliament elections in Poland and Hungary, Macron's message did not resonate there, even though the liberal and green parties in general experienced progress. Nevertheless, both PiS and Fidesz experienced even greater advances.

It has primarily fallen on the Commission to target both governments in letters and meetings and by launching several infringement cases against both countries. So far, it has had little success. A clear sign of the situation's increasing gravity is the European Commission's decision, in December 2017, to invoke Article 7 of the Lisbon Treaty against Poland. Article 7 states that voting rights in the Council of Minsters may be suspended if a member state repeatedly violates the values enumerated in Article 2 of the Lisbon Treaty, so that the state's behavior constitutes a "clear risk of systematic and repeated breach of basic democratic principles."[8] However, since unanimity among the heads of state and government is required, this so-called "nuclear bomb" is in reality unfeasible.

The European Parliament has been active when it comes to criticizing and questioning democratic lapses in some Eastern European states. It also suggested, on September 12, 2018, that EU leaders – who in any case have the final say – invoke Article 7 against Hungary. This move was triggered by a devastating report on the rule of law situation in Hungary issued by the Dutch MEP Judith Sargentini.[9] And yet, despite overwhelming evidence of the deterioration of democracy, up to now, not much has happened. The European Parliament as a whole supported the introduction of an Article 7 procedure against Hungary, but the European People's Party (EPP), a European parliamentary faction that includes Orbán's Fidesz party, is divided. The EPP decided on March 20, 2019, to suspend Orbán's Fidesz party from the faction. However, it was not primarily the Sargentini report that was the cause, but the fact that Orbán in Hungary at that time ran a campaign against the then Commission President, Jean-Claude Juncker, who himself was an EPP member. The suspension was meant to last until after the European Parliament elections on May 26, 2019, and was then followed up by a "wise men's group" headed by the former Council President Herman Van Rompuy. Their job was to write yet another report on the situation in Hungary and suggest whether Fidez should be let back into the EPP as a full member or be thrown out altogether.

Of course, the suspension rather than exclusion of Fidesz to begin with was no coincidence. The EPP is the parliament's most powerful political group (with Angela Merkel's CDU/CSU among its ranks), and, especially with CSU and EPP chairman Manfred Weber, Orbán has long enjoyed if not popularity then at least great sympathy. The criticism of the EPP's handling of Orbán's increasingly autocratic rule has therefore been quite stunning, not least of Orbán's success in calming the waters and keeping his EPP membership intact. The fact that there was an upcoming European Parliament election, and the fact that the EPP is a very powerful party group holding many influential posts in the EU have clearly been crucial. Excluding Fidesz was simply too risky and the appetite for losing an ally at that crucial moment just wasn't there.[10] Being the largest political group has resulted in privileges and great influence. For example, it was hoped that it would be possible to enforce the Spitzenkandidat process, thus ensuring that the EPP Spitzenkandidat became the Commission President. This partly succeeded, but not with Manfred Weber as the new President. Instead, the office went to German Defense Minister Ursula von der Leyen, who also belongs to the group. The crucial point here is, however, that it was clearly the EPP's internal reasoning that settled Orbán's suspension instead of exclusion.

Manfred Weber's role in the decision to "only" suspend Orbán has triggered massive criticism among independent lawyers who closely follow the developments in Hungary. It can be interpreted as a token of how we are increasingly losing the sense of what is right and wrong when it comes to democracy.

Few believe that Hungary or Poland could possibly meet the EU's democracy requirements were they applying for membership today. This makes it all the more alarming and incomprehensible that so few dare raise their voices now.

On several occasions in recent years in Warsaw and Budapest ordinary citizens, wearing blue flags with yellow stars, have demonstrated against their own governments. Here, civil society feels disappointed, not just by the EU, but also by the multiple Western voices that previously championed liberal values, human rights, and democracy, but at present remain silent. It is undoubtably ordinary citizens who pay the highest price for the doldrums. Before a discussion of how this could happen and why this must be seen as a result of our changed understandings of what democracy is, we must examine the underlying reasons why Poland and Hungary – so far – have been treated differently by the EU institutions and in particular the Commission.

There are immense differences in the European institutions' current approaches to these two members. The Polish PiS government has been far less fortunate than Orbán, because PiS is a member of the more controversial ECR (European Conservatives and Reformists) group, previously the home of the British Tories and also the Danish People's Party. Orbán's attacks on the judiciary, the press, and civil society have been more severe than those of Poland, and yet Poland has been treated far more harshly, even by EU institutions.

The crucial point to understand here is that – at the end of the day – it is the heads of state and government who must react to the drift to illiberalism in Europe. But apart from Macron, EU leaders have been unengaged.

Commentators chalk this up to leaders' fears of winding up in critical situations of their own and eventually needing the support of their friends and colleagues. If this is so, then looking the other way could be a deliberate strategy.[11] Politicians' silence when it comes to defending European values may also be another example of the rising fear of imposing a "politically correct" Western European view on democracy (if such a thing exists). This may sound perplexing, but one cannot rule it out as an excuse, however ill-informed, even inept, for failing to stand up for the Union's basic values and democratic standards.[12]

If this last explanation is even remotely true, then the sweep of populism across the continent may mark a changing definition of what democracy is and should be. And indeed, it is becoming more and more common to equate democracy with the decisions of an elected majority, irrespective of how much they contravene classic ideas of liberal democracy. According to this perspective, the people's choices are always democratic – even when they are not. If a majority votes for a politician like Orbán (for the third time!), the people's choice is legitimate and democratic even if he has employed his power to dismantle democracy itself. It may resemble a tautology, but the point is that if we accept the premise that democracy without the rule of law is a "real" democracy, we risk passively observing democracies elect themselves out of existence, as the British professor and philosopher Manjeet Ramgotra hinted in a recent article on illiberal democracy with the question: "Can democracy vote itself out of existence?"[13] The answer is yes, it can. And democracies are currently doing so – right before our eyes.

We may well end up in a situation where we legitimize elections that are only free in appearance. However, if our only criteria for democracy are formally holding an election and "winning the majority" while political opponents must make do with no media access, in an electoral system that disadvantages them, then voters are *not* making a free, enlightened choice. A country on this model will be democratic in name only, as Jan-Werner Müller has pointed out.[14]

The conflation of formal voting and unlimited majorities with democracy is spreading. China, Turkey, and Russia are all examples of countries that have elections, but few would argue that they are democracies. Russia especially, with Putin in front, has been a great inspirer, friend, and partner of Viktor Orbán. However, the important point is that our gradual acceptance of a formal election campaign as sufficient to legitimize democracy may be one of the main reasons for our inability to see what is happening before our eyes in these years and to defend our own European values.

I will look further into this as we dig deeper into what is happening to democracy in Europe. My argument is that if we cannot mobilize *conceptually* against the authoritarians in our midst, Europe has in many ways already succumbed to tribalism.

The tribalization we are witnessing is thus not just about identity politics in the narrow sense. It is also about an increasingly skewed understanding of what democracy means and should mean in a time of populism. This is true for all three cases discussed so far: the Catalan independence movement, the Brexiteers' campaign to leave the EU, and the Orbán–Kaczyński anti-democratic crusade. Each is a symptom of a Europe that is unraveling. Tribalization has already influenced how we perceive democracy today, defining downward the basic requirements for its presence.

Who Cares About
Democracy?

It is now commonplace for populists to refer to the will of the people when attempting to add greater force and authority to their own opinions. Less remarked upon is how many mainstream politicians, tainted by populist ideas and claims, have followed in their footsteps, gradually renouncing the liberal conception of democracy. "What the people want" is more and more often equated with democracy, irrespective of what safeguards are in place. In Brexit, among Catalan separatists, and in Orbán's endless tirades against the liberal elite and immigrants, what the people have allegedly voted for is supposedly what matters. However, the wave of populism with the people at the center has also been accompanied by a notion that democracy is most genuine when the will of the people is unlimited by other institutions, since these, because they do not reflect the will of the people, are elitist. Therefore, referenda are increasingly regarded as the optimal form of decision-making. This was evident in Catalonia in 2017, in the Brexit vote in 2016, and when Orbán again

Who Cares About Democracy?

and again uses questionnaires sent directly to the people as a way to defend his "reforms."

Even among political theorists, there has been a growing sympathy for – if not referenda – then majoritarian thinking in recent years, with a concomitant denunciation of strong counter-majoritarian institutions.[1] Prominent in this debate are British Professor of Political Science Richard Bellamy and American Professor of Political Science and Law Ran Hirschl. This debate is in many ways in contradiction to the one that has dominated Europe since the Nurnberg Laws, when most nations in Europe and beyond turned to constitutional democracy. Contrary to majoritarian democracy, constitutional democracy institutionalizes a solid judicial control with parliamentary majorities at any given time. Bellamy and Hirschl question whether it is justified – as the constitutionalists argue – to limit the political majority by non-elected bodies such as courts. This question is, of course, perfectly fair, and the question of how much power non-majoritarian institutions should have in a democracy is, of course, legitimate. But can a democracy really survive today – as a democracy – without such basic elements as constitutions, respect for minorities, and institutions that place limits on the will of the majority? And if it can, should we let it?

Figuratively, one can divide the different types of democracy in the manner shown in figure 1.

In this second half of the book we will look at the state of democracy today. We will show how populism and tribalism are gradually questioning and thus undermining the legitimacy of one of the central pillars of the post-Second World War order: counter-majoritarian institutions. Seen from a historical perspective, things

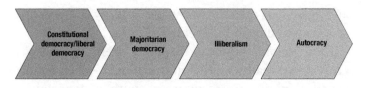

Figure 1   Different types of democracy

don't look so bad, however. In 2019, the world clearly had more democracies than in 1944. If we go all the way back to 1800 and take a broader perspective, the global trends are similarly encouraging. (See figure 2. While democracies and autocracies are well known categories, anocracies are regimes that are unstable and mix democratic with strong autocratic features.[2])

And yet, homing in on the past ten years' developments, things appear far less bright. According to the Economist Intelligence Unit, eighty-nine countries regressed democratically in 2017, while only twenty-seven improved.[3] According to the V-Dem project that I

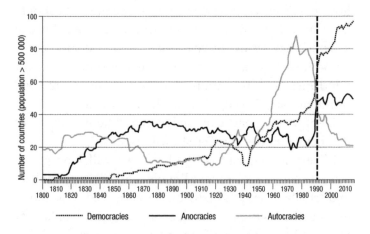

Figure 2   Global trends in governance, 1800–2016
Source: Center for Systemic Peace, Polity 5

cited in the introduction to this book, six of the countries
that have regressed from democracy are in Europe.

Moreover, a study from the Pew Research Centre
showed that 26 percent of those young people surveyed
no longer even value democracy over authoritarianism.[4]
The decline is supported by data from Mounk and
Foa[5] showing that among young millennials in America
in particular, only 30 percent today think that it is
important to live in a democracy, and this tendency can,
these researchers argue, be generalized to other Western
democracies as well. As they put it: "In virtually all
cases, the generation gap is striking, with the proportion
of younger citizens who believe it is essential to live in a
democracy falling to a minority."[6] Data also suggest that
rising income is no longer associated with a favorable
attitude toward democracy to which we have become
accustomed. We may thus have to say goodbye to the old
chestnut, favored among political scientists, that once an
income rises to $14,000 per capita, the risk of backsliding
into authoritarianism is low, as the German-American
political scientist Yascha Mounk put it in the *Economist*.[7]

Figures 3 and 4 show the overall rise in income levels
per capita in Europe and the rest of the world.

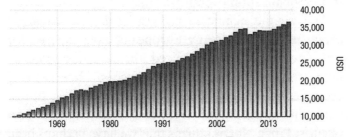

Figure 3   Rise in per capita income in Europe, 1960–2018
Source: Trading Economics, "European Union GDP per
capita 1960–2018"

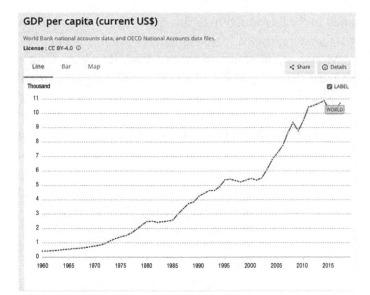

Figure 4   GDP per capita (current USD), 1961–2017
Source: World Bank, "GDP per capita (current US$)"

Obviously not everyone has gained equally from globalization and inequality remains a significant problem even in well-off Western societies, but studies also show middle-income groups have gained most from globalization overall (see figure 5).[8]

And yet the significant growth levels and rising per capita income that many Europeans have experienced seem not to have immunized them against identity politics and authoritarian demagogues. Here theories grounded in political science have proven weak. In line with the foregoing observations, American political scientist Pippa Norris affirms that we have perhaps been far too occupied with explaining the rise in populism by economic inequality. According to Norris, the median

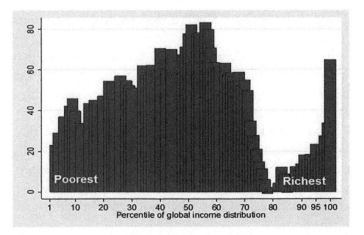

Figure 5   Cumulative real growth rate, 1988–2008
Source: B. Milanovic, "The Tale of Two Middle Classes," July 31, 2014, YaleGlobal, published by the MacMillan Center at Yale: https://yaleglobal.yale.edu/content/tale-two-middle-classes

Trump voter earns $10,000 more per year than the median American. There is thus little evidence that the preference for a populist leader like Trump is confined to lower-income groups. Authoritarian populism in the US and in Europe is a matter of culture, Norris argues.[9] When the white middle class voted for Trump, this was due primarily to a sense of being overlooked and pushed aside by the liberal left and minority groups fighting for LBGTQ rights and racial and gender equality. That it has become "the culture, stupid" (rather than "the economy, stupid" as the American President Bill Clinton's strategist once put it) that matters also seemed clear at the British general election in December 2019. Here Boris Johnson managed to pull off the biggest victory for the Tories since Margaret

Thatcher on his "get Brexit done" agenda despite years of austerity.

Irrespective of the root causes, few thus disagree that we are experiencing a revolt against liberal values and democracy impossible to foresee when we celebrated the fall of the Berlin Wall thirty years ago.

Examining the fragility of contemporary democracy, the challenges it faces, the question arises: who really cares? Not average voters, to all appearances. Fewer and fewer of them bother going to the polls, which is yet another sign of a declining trust in traditional institutions.

In the US, voter turnout for presidential elections has ranged since 2000 from 54.2 percent to 61.6 percent of the electorate; for congressional elections, the numbers are 35.9 percent and 41.0 percent since 2002.[10] This is hardly impressive in a country that regards itself as the land of the free.

Americans are not the only ones not showing up to vote. European democracies have experienced an overall decline in turnout over time. Participation peaked between the 1940s and 1980s, but since the 1990s, turnout has decreased significantly. One explanation lies with differences between Western and Eastern Europe. While average turnout across post-Communist countries has declined by around 20 percent since the break with Communism at the end of the 1980s, the decline among so-called established Western democracies was about 10 percent in the same period. It is important to note that this 10 percent decline started from a higher base. One explanation is the growing disenchantment with liberal democracy and its values as such, along with possible disappointment over the hardship many Central and

Eastern European countries experienced during their transition. Across Europe, however, attitudes toward democracy significantly affect voter behavior.[11]

Average turnout in the past five years in Europe, based on thirty-eight elections, has been 62.46 percent. Comparing this to the first five years of the 1990s, when average turnout, based on twenty-eight elections, was 77.45 percent, the decline is quite clear (see figure 6).

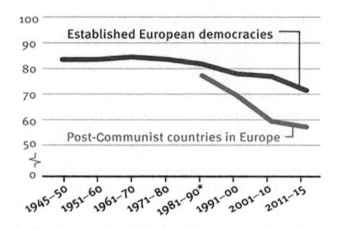

Figure 6   Voter turnout, 1945–2015
Note: *The first post-Cold War elections in post-Communist countries were held during 1989–90. Poland held its first post-Cold War election in 1989, and ten other countries followed in 1990. Data for the elections held in Poland and Yugoslavia before the end of the Cold War are included in the voter turnout data (VTD). There are no data in the VTD for elections held in the countries of the former Eastern bloc, the former Soviet Union, or the former Yugoslavia before 1990. Source: A. Solijonov, Voter Turnout Trends Around the World, International Institute for Democracy and Electoral Assistance (International IDEA), Stockholm (2016). https://www.idea.int/publications/catalogue/voter-turnout-trends-around-world

In regional and local elections, there are often even fewer who care to go to the ballots, though this varies from country to country and region to region. The reluctance to participate and engage in smaller-scale elections is widespread in the US as well as in Europe.

In European Parliament elections in spring 2019 the turnout was 50.1 percent, which was 8.34 percent higher than in 2014.

In 2014 the post-Communist countries were at the low end in that election too, with only 13 percent voter turnout in Slovakia and 18 percent in the Czech Republic! Both countries increased their voter turnout in 2019 and reached respectively 22.74 percent and 28.72 percent. In 2014 the UK also hit bottom, however; only 35.6 percent cared to show up to cast their vote. In 2019 the story stays the same: 37 percent voted, but with the enormous difference that because of the unresolved Brexit issue the British were suddenly forced to participate in the European Parliament elections. The election and campaigns were therefore not very well prepared. Although the European elections had a relatively high voter turnout in 2019 and resulted in a defeat for the right-wing alliance of Italian Interior Minister Matteo Salvini, there is no doubt that many voters still see the European Parliament as less important and influential than national parliaments.[12] In many countries, the European elections are perceived as "second-order" elections, where voters tend to focus on national issues and to use the European parliamentary elections to send a message (often of dissatisfaction) to national politicians instead of actively engaging with European topics.[13]

Despite the decreasing numbers of people who vote in both national and European elections, it is increasingly

Who Cares About Democracy?

common to hear newly elected leaders say they speak on behalf of the people. But who are they really, the people?

Who Are The People?

Political scientist Yascha Mounk argues in his book *The People vs. Democracy* that equating the will of the people with democracy is problematic and puts democracy itself at risk. Democracy was never just about voting, or referendum-style voting restricted to one single issue. Democracy is a balancing of political objectives – in particular when it comes to difficult questions that may have serious consequences for an entire community for decades.

Nevertheless as established institutions and liberal democracy face an increasing number of challenges, and the will of the people continues to be invoked whenever any new populistic political proposal arises, it is worth asking the basic question: who are "the people"?

Should we define the people as those who show up to vote on election day, even when only a minority of the electorate makes use of its right to make its voice heard? Or are the people everyone, regardless of who shows up? Newly elected presidents and heads of state rarely miss the opportunity to say they represent "the entire people" – including those who either didn't care to vote or voted for another candidate – when they give their first speech. While this statement is not entirely false, it is certainly debatable whether "the people" encompasses in any meaningful way those who – for different reasons – abstained from casting their vote. Those who stay home as a protest, because they don't endorse the candidates on offer or don't want to be included in the crowd that a new leader claims to speak for – are they, too, the people? And do they wish to be regarded as such?

This question of who the people really are becomes even more complex when we discuss referenda. What does a plebiscite tell us? Does the result speak for the entire people when the winning majority is a very narrow yes or no? Few Remainers in the Brexit debacle would likely care to be included in the oft-repeated statement, "The British people have spoken and want out of the EU." The turnout for the Brexit vote was relatively high, 72.2 percent, but, as we know, only 52 percent wanted to leave the EU. Are the 48 percent who wanted to stay then also to be regarded as "the people?" In addition, what happens when very few show up to vote? Should the outcome still be considered legitimate and as representing "the people"?

We saw exactly that in the Catalan independence vote on October 1, 2017, after which the leader of the independence movement, Carles Puigdemont, was quick to conclude that the Catalan people wanted to break away from Spain. However, only 43 percent of those eligible to vote actually showed up at the ballots. Even if 92 percent voted yes, 43 percent was still a minority. This important point is often skipped over.

Who Are The People?

The question of how to define the demos or the people can be (and is) easily misused. What if – as suggested earlier – the majority in Barcelona decided to leave Catalonia and remain in Spain? Would the separatists' logic embrace such a scenario? As the Danish political theorist Christian Rostbøll eloquently states:

> Does the democratic self-determination argument imply that any group, region, or city has a right to secede or create its own country? Would Barcelona or Val d'Aran be allowed to leave an independent Catalonia? It seems to me that self-determination arguments are never only: "the people should decide for themselves." There is always another argument at play concerning who counts as a people – and this argument is not an argument from democracy.[1]

Who the people are is not only a matter of the numbers taking part in a plebiscite or a national election (which in some countries is even mandatory). It is also not to be defined from the winning majority. It is a question of rules and institutions as well.

And yet, in the Brexit debate and the debate on Catalonian independence, we heard the same thing over and again: "The people have spoken, and we should respect their will" to (a) exit the EU or (b) secede from Spain. In both cases it is permissible to wonder whether the result of these two votes truly represented the will of the Catalan or the British people.

Viktor Orbán, too, has cannily marshaled the Hungarian demos to legitimize his policies. On a number of occasions, he has used surveys distributed to Hungarian households directly to make it easier to

confirm his own pet policies; for example, to demon-
strate that "the people" of Hungary would never accept
mandatory reallocation of Muslim migrants or even a
common European migration policy.[2]

This trick of reducing the will of the people to
referenda or more or less ridiculous surveys, discarding
all other democratic procedures and institutions is
dangerous not only because it polarizes political debate,
as in Brexit and the Catalan referendum. There is a
deeper problem that lies in the very concept of the referendum, and also in the ways it has been used.

Plebiscite democracy is deeply divisive and alien to the
basic principles of modern representative democracy, in
which politicians are elected to take difficult decisions
with long-term consequences.

Putting critical questions to the vote can become an
excuse for avoiding the headaches of pursuing a difficult
agenda through customary representative institutions.
Former British Prime Minister David Cameron is the
prime example of a leader who chose to solve internal
party problems through a referendum: the referendum on
remaining in the European Union in 2016. He believed
– naïvely – that allowing his EU-skeptic backbenchers
(and the aging Tory party members) to vote on Brexit
would calm their irascibility. He also believed that
"remain" would win an overwhelming victory, but
forgot to plan what the consequences of a "leave" vote
might be. Therefore, the subsequent Brexit shock was a
sudden awakening for Cameron, for the entire political
establishment, and for the Brexit side itself, whose
members had not thought that they actually could win.
We now know that the British referendum didn't mend
existing rifts – if anything, three years and two general

elections later, they have likely gotten worse. This is true not only among the British Conservatives, but in British society as a whole, particularly between generations and between the different nations that constitute "the United Kingdom."

Have we learned anything from all of this then? Perhaps that supporters of plebiscites would do well to consider building in some security mechanisms or thresholds, not only to protect the losing minority, but also to assure that a minimum percentage of eligible voters must take part and vote in favor for the result to be valid. Harvard Professor Kenneth Rogoff drives this point home in his account of the incredibly low threshold the UK set for leaving the EU, despite the consequences for generations to come:

> The real lunacy of the United Kingdom's vote to leave the European Union was not that British leaders dared to ask their populace to weigh the benefits of membership against the immigration pressures it presents. Rather, it was the absurdly low bar for exit, requiring only a simple majority. Given voter turn out of 70% this meant that the leave campaign won with only 36% of eligible voters backing it.[3]

Another possibility would have been a promise from the outset of a second vote once the deal the EU offered the UK was presented. Thus, the extremely divided British people could have been promised that once the deal that Britain would negotiate with the EU was unambiguous, voters would be asked if this was what they really wanted. Holding a general election between two referenda was another possibility, especially for an issue of sufficient gravity – which Brexit no doubt was and still is. Finally, there could have been a generational weighting of the vote, with more sway given to members of younger generations, who will have to live with the outcome for decades to come.

In the illegal Catalan independence referendum, the threshold was even lower, because many eligible voters chose not to show up. The generational factor was important here as well. Any potential legal vote on Catalan independence in the future will undoubtedly affect millions of people, including beyond Catalonia's borders.

When dealing with complex decisions that have long-lasting consequences, a simple yes/no vote risks alienating that part of the demos that winds up in the minority, and may easily rob future generations of their dreams and aspirations. Let us return to the Catalan case, which has much to say about this particular quandary.

The Purpose of a Constitution

The Catalan referendum on October 1, 2017, is a good example of what can happen when asking the people is used as a tool for political activism. Several questions about democratic legitimacy came to the fore in this turbulent vote on independence. Even the path to decide on holding a referendum in the Catalan parliament caused a huge stir, as it was known to be a breach of the Spanish constitution. Only after an eleven-hour debate, with fifty-two opposition members departing the negotiations in protest, did former Catalan President Carles Puigdemont get his vote through parliament.

The separatists were clearly not very concerned about the legality of the vote (whether under Spanish or international law), nor did they care how few participated on October 1, 2017.[1] Thus the entire exercise seemed first and foremost a spectacle mocked up for an already sympathetic international audience.

What does the Spanish constitution actually say? As in other democracies, it prohibits regional authorities from holding referenda on issues of national import, the results of which would constitute de facto amendment to the constitution.² A region thus cannot unilaterally declare itself an independent state. This should probably come as no surprise to anyone with even remote knowledge of constitutional theory and has been twice confirmed by the Spanish Constitutional Court. As described in the chapter on "Tribal Thinking and Dreams of Detachment," it would not be legal according to international law either.

We must remember that one of the primary purposes of a constitution is to create stability and avoid sudden popular moods (or moody politicians!) overturning the social contract and reaping immense societal and generational consequences. This does not mean that people are not allowed to air their opinion about an issue or to campaign for a new independent state – or indeed a new constitution. In a democracy, everyone has freedom of speech.

Could the Spanish government's response to the illegal Catalan referendum then have been more elegant? As the referendum was mainly produced for international media consumption, the Spanish government could have chosen just to ignore it. Such a reaction was probably impossible but the severity of Madrid's reaction, which included closing election sites and physically preventing people from casting their votes, was no doubt welcomed by Puigdemont and his people. They exploited the rather harsh reaction to garner additional support and media attention outside the country. The end result was thus exactly what Puigdemont had wanted: his movement appeared as the victims fighting a relentless oppressive power. Puigdemont and the separatists managed, thanks in part to the rather disastrous handling of the revolt by the Spanish authorities, to present the international media with a narrative of a small, marginalized culture crushed by an authoritarian government – almost like Francoist Spain. It is important to note, however, that even though the conservative government did a very bad public relations job and the following trials and imprisonments of the separatist revolutionaries were condemned by many outside Spain, few today question that Spain is a stable democracy with a strong rule of law tradition. And Spain still figures as a full democracy in the Economist Intelligence Unit's yearly scoreboard – something not all European countries, as we have seen, can boast of.[3]

The separatists – and certainly those who ended up in jail – were less pleased when they learned their former leader Carles Puigdemont had fled the country to escape the responsibility for a vote of which he had been the main architect.

Two points are important here when the discussion is about populism and tribal thinking in a slightly broader perspective, and thus relevant in the multiple contexts where populist leaders repeatedly claim to speak on behalf of the people. The first, already emphasized many times, is simply: who are the people of Catalonia? Is there any meaning to the argument that the Catalans want independence when only a minority chose to cast their vote in an independence referendum? Are those who stayed home not more representative of the Catalans than the minority who actually went out to vote? Perhaps the answer lies somewhere in between. This leads me to my second point, which pertains to the legitimacy of a unilateral Catalan vote on independence.

If we put the illegality of the vote aside for a moment, does one regional constituency then have a moral right to take the fundamental, probably irreversible decision to break up an entire country? Or should letting a region go be a decision taken in common by the whole of (in this case) Spain? Surely not only the Catalans themselves are concerned about a possible detachment of Catalonia from Spain. Many Spanish citizens outside Catalonia have a strong attachment to the region; many have family, friends, and ancestors from there. Take a trip to Madrid or Barcelona and bring up the topic at a bar and you will have no doubt how much this issue concerns any Spaniard. Leaving citizens outside Catalonia without a say in its future is certainly questionable. One could perhaps consider transferring the contrasting principle of the Good Friday Agreement to the Spanish case in any future discussion on independence. The Good Friday agreement of 1999 created peace in Northern Ireland and at the same time mandated that any possible future unification of Ireland and Northern Ireland was conditional on a positive supportive referendum in *both* territories.

Getting back to Spain, it is also important to remember that the half of the Catalan population that does not want to leave Spain would – in case of a legal vote in favor of independence – stand to lose much more than just their Spanish citizenship. They also risk losing their European Union citizenship with all the rights attached as well, as there is no guarantee that Catalonia would automatically become a new member of the European Union. Rather the opposite; especially if the detachment takes place without Spanish consent. These are huge but often overlooked consequences.

Declaring Catalonia an independent state would also affect and question Spain's status as a sovereign nation. This is another, less discussed reason why Madrid likely showed so little hesitation in invoking Article 155 of the Spanish constitution after the independence vote in 2017. By doing so, the Spanish government rescinded local authorities' right to self-rule and introduced direct rule from the capital.

A declaration of independence would thus constitute a fundamental disregard for the Spanish constitution itself, adopted democratically and by a large majority (not least in Catalonia) in 1978. This document, which replaced the Franco regime's constitution, forbids – as mentioned earlier – regional referenda that call into question the legal foundations of the country.[4] Law professor Javier García Oliva, in an article on Catalonia, describes constitutions' importance as basic safeguards of stability: "when matters are decided by popular vote, there will often be winners and losers, but constitutions exist, to an extent, precisely in order to safeguard the interests of the losers, and the importance of this should not be underestimated."[5] Constitutions may in other words contain political impulses and prevent disasters.

This does not mean that a constitution cannot be changed with the backing of a sufficient majority. It has recently been suggested that a less confrontational, more pragmatic solution to the Catalan problem could be the adoption of a federal model for Spain as a whole. Catalonia is already a *Comunidad Autónoma*, a kind of sub-state within Spain, and has greater autonomy than many other Spanish regions, including greater control of its linguistic policy, healthcare system, and social and education policies than most regions in Europe.[6]

Pursuit of a federal agenda would, however, require separatists to abandon their identitarian agenda and rhetoric. Unfortunately, the likelihood of this happening is minimal, since it is precisely the identitarian project that keeps the separatist elite's project ignited and in power.[7] Still, illegal referenda and media sideshows are not the way forward in the separatists' pursuit of reform. It is, moreover, doubtful that the idea of independence and ethnocultural propaganda will continue to garner support outside Spain's borders in the long run.

While referenda may look like quick fixes to dilemmas of whether to stay or leave a union (Brexit) or a state (Catalan separatists), they neither provide long-term solutions nor secure social and generational cohesion.

* * *

In a tribalist world in which the answers to complex societal challenges are often presented in simplistic language, referenda are widely and loudly praised. But the increased resort to plebiscites is not the only or even the most important problem facing liberal democracies. A greater challenge is the extreme majoritarianism that has won more and more supporters in recent years and which often is accompanied by a crusade against anti-majoritarian institutions. While democracies used to boast of their protection of minorities, control of state power, and free press, extreme majoritarian systems often maintain the trappings of democracy. These do hold elections, but there are no or very few de facto limits constraining people in power. At the point where counter-majoritarian institutions are largely dismantled, we have moved beyond what one meaningfully could call democracy. When this happens, governing bodies have already taken control of the courts and often limited the free press and civil society in a piecemeal fashion.

While this may look like a description of Europe in the 1930s, it is in fact a depiction of parts of Europe today. That we have come this far almost without noticing it is due not only to the gathering wave of populism but also to gradually changing ideas about what defines democracy. However, it may also be attributed to receding self-confidence among liberal democracy's erstwhile defenders. Many of the latter have taken a lax approach to the current undermining of the rule of law. Some are so busy lamenting their own mistakes and analysis as they overlooked the anger that led to Trump and Brexit that they almost cheer dictator types, like Orbán, on to power. Apparently, we should tolerate and champion those who, after forty years behind the Iron Curtain, now finally have the courage to stand by their own "special" version of democracy. However, this is not only misunderstanding democracy. It is also being blind to the clear and present dangers we are currently facing. This tendency is, moreover, unsettling, as it is frequently accompanied by a hesitation to criticize, intervene in, and forcefully counter the waves of autocracy that are flooding not only the world in general but specifically part of the European continent. Should the lack of discussion of these developments among media people and political organizations not be interpreted as silent consent or at least toleration? In a place like Europe, which has been the home of some of the world's most heinous atrocities as well as the most comprehensive human rights regime, Article 2 of the EU Treaty should not be up for debate. The European values and the very foundation of the rule of law cannot (and should not) be bent with reference to a particular "cultural understanding" of what democracy is. At least not if you want to be part of the Europe we have jointly built, with a common treaty based on liberal ideals. Still, one might wonder how weak the defenses are for these particular values. As Larry Diamond, researcher in democracy, puts it: "when what the autocrats see is Western apathy, of course they will calculate that there is plenty of room to go as far as is needed."[8] When commentators and politicians remain silent (or worse still, "understanding") in the debate about what "can be tolerated" within the framework of liberal democracy, it is a tacit acceptance that democracy and the rule of law are always up for discussion. But are we willing to accept the degradation of democracy in some places to something that approaches or already constitutes autocracy? Ask the youngsters in the streets of current Hong Kong what they think, or the people in the streets of Warsaw, Prague, Valetta, Budapest, or Bratislava.

In parts of current Europe liberal principles are already things of the past. How did their disappearance go unnoticed? Let us now turn to this.

Democracy Without Limits?

When the US ratified its constitution in 1788, checks and balances between the different branches of government were among its central tenets. American democracy was held in check by a strong Supreme Court that soon acquired the power to overrule Congress and even the President if either was in breach of the constitution, as established in the landmark Marbury v. Madison case of 1803. In *Democracy in America* (1831) Alexis de Tocqueville enthusiastically described how the judicial control of politicians had become one of the most important symbols of American democracy. It signaled that the constitution is always primary, that everyone is equal before the law, and that independent judges and courts are the principal defenders of the basic rules of democracy. Tocqueville described the judges as the *true guardians of liberty* and emphasized how Europeans too should assimilate the central role of the courts in the new American democracy. He warned against any attempt by "the people to reduce the power of the judiciary," as he puts it: "I venture to predict that these innovations will have, sooner or later, disastrous results and it will be seen that an attack has been directed against not only the power of judges but against the democratic republic itself."[1] Judges were able, Tocqueville argued, to actively protect the individual against the state by setting aside legislation that encroaches on individual liberties. The courts are not just "custodians of the law," but a true "counter-majoritarian" force limiting the President as well as the majority in Congress when necessary. These principles were, however, unknown in most European countries at the time.

In Europe before the Second World War, most parliamentary systems had no significant and strong counter-majoritarian institutions. More or less unlimited majority rule was the norm on the continent, where democracy was still young. Even today, majority rule is perceived as intuitively more democratic in many places. Democracy, after all, means "rule by the people" in Greek. Especially in Britain and Scandinavia the idea that democracy has always and primarily been about "counting seats" and establishing a majority in parliament is to this day still maintained with great fondness. Accordingly, because it represents the "people," parliament should preferably not be decisively restricted by unelected anti-majoritarian institutions, that is by courts with strong review powers. What consequences this has and has had, I will return to below. The point is that the protection of the individual and of minorities against the tyranny of the majority was not something that was of particular concern at that time.

Of course, it is not entirely true that the Europeans only after the Second World War adopted the important idea of limiting political power. Since the Magna Carta[2] it has been judged necessary to put in place mechanisms to protect people from abuse by their rulers. And yet it was only after the Second World War and the atrocities committed against Jews and other minorities by the Nazis that most Europeans saw a need to introduce serious checks on parliaments.

"Constitutionalism" entailing exactly this new instrument became the new buzzword in postwar Europe. The recognition of the need to "limit the power of the majority" has subsequently been named the "Nuremberg Moment." Constitutional democracy, with its emphasis on protecting and promoting the new European constitutions and human rights, replaced most – but not all – majoritarian democracies in Europe. Constitutional democracy is more formally understood as institutionalizing a "form of *liberal* democracy where parliaments are counter-balanced by relatively strong judicial review mechanisms."[3] This new way of understanding democracy thus triumphed in the aftermath of the war as a reaction to the lack of judicial checks and protection of basic rights under the Weimar Republic. The German Nuremberg Laws, which deprived Jews and other ethnic minorities of a wide range of civil rights, were accepted by the parliamentary majority of the German Reichstag, which was not limited by a strong constitution and constitutional court that could (or would) have declared the laws void and against all human decency. The establishment of a strong German Constitutional Court after the war was in many ways a direct reaction to the weak republic, which had not been able to forestall the slaughter of millions of innocent people.

The limits on majorities and governments after the Second World War were further buttressed by reciprocal commitments established through international treaties and conventions at the global and European level. This led to the Universal Declaration of Human Rights in 1948 and the adoption of the European Convention on Human Rights in 1950. It was thought urgent to develop a more binding set of rules *beyond the state level* to protect human rights after the war and the drastic failure of Woodrow Wilson's League of Nations in the interwar period.[4]

The "constitutional revolution" was in other words a twofold phenomenon affecting individual countries and Europe as a whole, which had the additional aim of building up a bulwark against Communism. However, it took a long time before human rights became a part of the EU treaties. After the war and with the establishment of the Coal and Steel Community and later the Treaty of Rome, the work was divided: the Council of Europe (the intergovernmental body attached to the Convention and the Strasbourg Court) took care of human rights while the "EC" – the European Community – took care of economic cooperation. Of course the Community had its four freedoms and basic principles of national non-discrimination but these were, at least to begin with, mainly aimed at making the single "market" function as smoothly as possible. It was only gradually and much later that the EU – through the case law of the European Court of Justice and in the treaties (with the charter of fundamental rights) – developed its own human rights and rule of law principles.

After the Second World War the German *national* constitutional revolution soon spread beyond Germany, first to Italy and later to most other European states, which freed themselves from authoritarianism and adopted new constitutions.[5] As Shapiro and Stone Sweet put it: "[T]he rights and review tandem [became] an essential, even obligatory, component of any move toward constitutional democracy" in Europe in these years.[6]

But the constitutional revolution in Europe did not stop there. After the breakup of the Soviet Union, the new democracies of Central and Eastern Europe abandoned Communism while acquiring basic counter-majoritarian institutions. Before the EU, with its Copenhagen criteria, association agreements, and admission criteria, demanded it, Poland and Hungary adopted constitutions that included strong courts and checks and balances. Thus, there was a clear desire to embrace constitutionalism – at least among the new elite who helped transform these societies into democracies. Of course, the wish to "become as in the West" as soon as possible, as Ivan Krastev has pointed out, was profound, but there was also the long-term objective of joining the EU. Interestingly, the impending enlargement was also one of the reasons why Western Europe and the EU began to focus on human rights in the EU treaties, which had otherwise – as mentioned above – had a very economic focus. Already in the 1990s, however, the German Constitutional Court had criticized, in several so-called "Solange" judgments, the fact that the EU Court had declared the primacy of EU law *without* at the same time having an emphasis on the protection of human rights in the treaties. This could, according to the German Constitutional Court, mean that the far-reaching human rights protection that had entered the German constitution after the Second World War risked being rejected by the EU's top court, because the EU itself (and its treaties) did not guarantee the same human rights protection. This criticism that the EU was too focused on economics rather than values and human rights – along with the prospect of the inclusion of from eight to ten mainly post-Communist countries, most of which had fragile democratic traditions – was the primary reason for the EU to consider better safeguarding of human rights within the EU. The European Court of Justice therefore began to establish human rights in its case law. Later, the EU leaders introduced the "Charter of Fundamental Rights," on top of the Copenhagen criteria, which, with the Lisbon Treaty in 2009, finally entered the EU treaties.

These new mechanisms had barely managed to consolidate by 2010, when especially Hungary was already taking an anti-liberal turn. In 2015, Poland followed suit when the conservative PiS government came to power. Politicians in both countries have sought to remove the constraints on their parliamentarian majorities in recent years through so-called judicial reforms, curbing the power of the court and appointing their cronies to the bench.[7]

It should perhaps be noted that the current Hungarian and Polish governments have not been alone in their (new) distaste for strong counter-majoritarian institutions. While most countries after the Second World War decided to adopt checks by strong judicial bodies, some important democratic players – up to today, and even in Western Europe – have been skeptical about this development. In Great Britain and Denmark, one frequently hears that unelected judges should not have the power to override the will of the majority, particularly in the transnational or European context.

The UK and Denmark have traditionally belonged in this category, having for long cultivated the idea of sovereignty in parliament, with the presumption that parliament is elevated above other branches of government.[8] Both countries (like Sweden and Finland, where, until recently, judicial review has been directly banned in national constitutional laws) have rejected constitutional courts that actively and zealously monitor the legislature. The dislike of judicial and constitutional review has interestingly kept pace in this part of Europe with judges often being portrayed as an "unelected elite." Concurrently, if one could refer to the "people" (and thus the majority in parliament) in these countries one could virtually always trump any other argument. In a way, populism in today's version was modern here long before it became an international concept, if one understands populism as a way to consciously employ the "people" against a so-called "elite."

Research has moreover shown that countries with little or no tradition of strong judicial review powers at the national level will be more skeptical of international judicial bodies than countries that *do* have this experience at home.[9] This may help explain why the Luxembourg and Strasbourg courts have been under fire from the UK and Denmark in particular in recent years. These two countries' attempt to openly limit the power of the Strasbourg court through the Brighton and Copenhagen Declarations was clearly rooted in a majoritarian dislike of supranational courts that – in these countries' view – have too much discretion over national parliaments.[10] Their aim was to bring "human rights back home" (they have argued) and to let rights be decided by political forces and national courts rather than international courts.

The British concept of parliamentary sovereignty and the country's aversion to "unelected and unaccountable" international judges was also apparent in Theresa May's Lancaster speech on Brexit from January 17, 2017, where the European Court in Luxembourg was the target:

> [W]e will take back control of our laws and bring an end to the jurisdiction of the European Court of Justice in Britain. Leaving the European Union will mean that our laws will be made in Westminster, Edinburgh, Cardiff, and Belfast. And those laws will be interpreted by judges not in Luxembourg but in courts across this country.[11]

During the past years' Brexit spectacle even "elitist" *British* justices were the target, especially regarding Brexit-related decisions. On the front page of the *Daily Mail* on November 4, 2016, the headline was "Enemies of the People." Here, three justices were criticized for demanding that the British parliament was to be consulted in the British government's Brexit negotiations. The justices were also attacked by the Johnson government in September 2019 for their decision to declare the government's prorogation of parliament in the middle of the Brexit mess illegal.[12]

Could such an attack on courts and justices have happened ten or fifteen years ago, and should we see this and the Copenhagen and Brighton declarations as part of an increasing questioning of the international liberal order as such? It is hard to tell, but there is clearly an anti-multilateral and anti-constitutionalist instinct at play here. An instinct that may help us explain not only Brexit and the tribal tendencies that may manifest themselves in the future, but also the current challenges to the rule of law in Europe. It is, in other words, probably no coincidence that the only countries that initially supported the Danish desire to limit the power of the Strasbourg court were autocratic countries such as Russia and Hungary. In other words, it is naïve not to acknowledge that the ongoing delegitimization of international institutions that we are witnessing at present, and which contribute to destabilizing the international order that has created peace and prosperity in Europe since the Second World War, originate not only in the East but also in the West.

Ivan Krastev notes how independent institutions, like courts, central banks, and the media, are often the first to suffer when the liberal international order and democracy as such are called into question.[13]

The extreme majoritarianism we have seen growing in Hungary in particular over the past ten years thus clashes dramatically with the heritage of and the lessons learned from the Second World War, in which the Americans above all pushed for the establishment of counter-majoritarian institutions in exchange for Marshall Plan aid. For liberal democrats, democracy became inseparable from independent courts interpreting law and treaties and protecting human rights and minorities from the encroachment of majorities. This is also why, from a strictly constitutionalist perspective, courts should never be subject to the shifting moods of governing majorities or to the whims of the masses as expressed in elections. If this were to be the case, courts would no longer be independent, and would have lost their role as an impartial source of balance, as Montesquieu stressed in *The Spirit of the Laws*.[14]

Courts that are controlled by the political sphere thus *strongly* conflict with liberal democracy, as well as with the faith that a verdict reached by a court is objective and not influenced by other concerns. As I will discuss further in the next chapter, one of the more technical issues is that politically controlled courts exactly do create uncertainty as to whether a ruling is unaffected by political considerations. If courts are not independent and impartial, how can we be sure that they will enforce the rule of law for all rather than pursue a particular governing majority's interests? Thus, the balance of power and respect for the rule of law become the very test of whether a system is truly democratic.

* * *

Checks and balances as well as a non-politicized judiciary are quintessential to democracy.[15] Without independent judicial constraints on political majorities and a willingness to protect the individual against the state, a political system cannot properly be called a liberal democracy. This means that the government and those who answer to it cannot (and *should not*) be directly involved in the appointment of judges or in determining the length of their contracts, the timing of their promotions, their retirement age, or any other issues through which their impartiality might be threatened. Trying to influence or co-opt courts and prosecutors, or even merely slandering impartial judges as an "unelected elite" or "enemies of the people," represent a serious tribal shift away from liberal democracy and an attempt to arrogate power to one institution or person.

Understanding this is essential to grasping the situation not only in Poland and Hungary as I have discussed it throughout this book, but also in several other EU countries where democracy is growing weaker and corruption cases are multiplying.

The attempt to seize power over the judiciary was the reason why the Commission pushed ahead with the Article 7 case against Poland in July 2018.[16] The government attempted to legitimize this so-called judicial reform with the argument that an old guard of Communist judges had misused their powers. The government also claimed that the judges took power away from the people and their elected representatives in parliament. In April 2018, the government then introduced a new law lowering the retirement age of judges in the Polish Supreme Court, making a third of the judges eligible for retirement. Admittedly, the judges were able to "request" an extension from the government's judicial appointment board and thus remain in their positions, but this was ultimately not – as mentioned earlier – an impartial and professional decision, but a purely political one. When the judges subsequently refused to obey, members of civil society gathered in the streets of Warsaw to protest and show their support.

The attempt to politically manipulate the working conditions of the judiciary was such an obvious breach of the EU's (and indeed any democracy's) basic principles that the EU had no choice but to address it. Despite several years of continuous dialogue and warnings from the Commission, the Polish government and President

Duda refused to back down on the general reform. Several infringement cases were launched, just as the Polish judges themselves presented a case on the law's legality, or compatibility with EU law, before the European Court of Justice. The rather dramatic Article 7 procedure was thus only one tool of several, but one that, if successful, is able to deprive Poland of its voting rights on the Council. In addition to the Article 7 case, which is still waiting at the time of writing for the Council to take a position, the Commission has also initiated three "ordinary" infringement cases against Poland. These concern other parts of the reform, all of which have affected and changed the distribution of powers between politicians and lower-level judges.[17] Beyond these rather radical steps in Poland itself several lawsuits sought to reverse the reforms, and in December 2018, the European Court of Justice ordered the government to rehire the fired judges. Their forced retirement contravened European law and values and had to be addressed, the Court said.[18]

How has the Polish government then reacted to all this? So far, it has made some concessions as regards the retirement scheme and several judges are therefore back on the court. However, the government has not backed down on the creation of two new judicial chambers, one to discipline unruly judges, the other to review old rulings inimical to the government (and decide on the validity of future elections), and so it is still difficult to see that these concessions are substantive.[19]

While the cases against Poland and Hungary may seem complex and have spawned the usual criticism of elitist (supranational) judges and bureaucrats interfering in member states' internal (constitutional) affairs, it is absolutely essential for the EU's survival as a legitimate democratic institution that it does interfere. Indeed, thus far it has been too hesitant and has interfered too little – and perhaps too late.

Why is this so important? First because, if the EU is to continue calling itself a community governed by the rule of law, it cannot risk being seen as incapable of living up to its own standards. To avoid losing legitimacy, it must insist that everyone live up to the basic principles of democracy and the rule of law (including the Copenhagen criteria, which of course determined the eligibility for joining the Union).[20] Nor can (or should) large amounts of structural and agricultural funds be transferred to EU member states unless we are sure that the rules and national institutions preventing and prosecuting fraud and corruption are effectively supported and enforced. As the first Vice-President of the European Commission, Frans Timmermanns, put it when he was still in charge of fundamental rights: "The Union's capacity to uphold the rule of law is essential, now more than ever. First because it is an issue of fundamental values, a matter of 'who we are.' Second, because the functioning of the EU as a whole depends on the rule of law in all member states."[21]

Remember that the EU has been severe in applying sanctions to members that have fallen short of the Union's economic demands. Countries like Portugal, Ireland, and Greece were placed under conservatorship and turned into so-called "programme countries" during the financial crisis. It would thus be both ironic and difficult to explain to European citizens and future generations if the EU were to prove stricter in enforcing economic discipline than enforcing those democratic rules and values that everything else depend on.

Trust in member states' judicial systems is also essential for the smooth functioning of the internal market. If politicians take over the courts, whether directly or indirectly, judges in other member states will no longer be able to trust their peers. National courts in law-abiding states will stop collaborating with backlash states, and no longer dare to base their own decisions on cases decided in member states where the courts cannot be guaranteed to be independent.[22] Nor would businesses likely settle in countries where the judiciary is not sure to be impartial. In fact, if the EU does not stand up for its basic rules and values, the entire legal framework underpinning the single market – which firms, citizens, and governments rely on – may well be in jeopardy.

Finally, and significantly, the EU is also an international actor participating in a globalized world. For years, the EU has been busy lecturing others about democracy – not least in its "democracy for aid" programs. It would be almost comical if, in the future, the Union were to attempt to impose democratic conditions on its foreign policy and development partners while being incapable of following its own advice at home.[23] Not only authoritarian regimes like Turkey and Russia, but also developing African states where the EU for decades has made aid conditional on democratic development, will hardly listen to EU advice if the Union fails to insist on democracy within its own borders.

Why worry about all of this? As we are to see below in the Hungarian case, we have in many ways already crossed a red line when it comes to democratic backsliding in Europe. We seem to have silently accepted that member states may gradually dismantle democratic institutions without any consequences. As long as they hold elections, there is nothing to complain about, it seems.[24]

Hungary has not only eluded its European commitments but also influenced many others in Europe with its illiberal ideas. Although Orbán would like to portray himself as a persecuted innocence criticized by the EU – strangely enough, not for his undermining of the rule of law but always for his opposition to Muslim refugees – he has in reality carried out a coup d'état against liberal democracy without the use of tanks or weapons. By quietly transforming Hungarian society over the past ten years while only superficially addressing criticism from European institutions, Orbán has left the rest of the EU in a shambles. Those who pay the highest price for this are undoubtedly the Hungarian citizens and civil society, who, because the media is no longer free, have had difficulty navigating the political landscape. Orbán's tactics of increasing social benefits for pensioners and families with children (just as PiS does in Poland) have kept country-dwelling voters happy, in particular. At the same time, however, while EU leaders have hesitated to act, hundreds of thousands of Europeans have gathered in protest against corrupt and illiberal leaders in Bucharest, Prague, Warsaw, Budapest, and Bratislava.

This is encouraging. However, it is time we reminded ourselves of what democracy really is. Semi-authoritarian regimes in our midst have until now exploited our complacency, our naïve belief that as long as elections are held, few further safeguards are needed. There is no question that illiberal, anti-democratic sentiment has gained a foothold in Europe. The only question is whether it is already too late to do something about it.

Are Illiberal Democracies Democracies?

What do you do about countries that gradually and without anyone noticing it redefine liberal democracy and those principles they accepted when they became EU members? Are illiberal democracies even to be called democracies? And who is to define what a "true" democracy is? Many are soul-searching as they try to find the morally right answer to these questions. Below I will argue that yes, we have to take a stand on democracy and also to not be afraid of defining what we require for a society to be truly democratic.

Countries like Poland and Hungary have in recent years been moving away from liberal democracy. They have done so by removing constitutional and judicial constraints on their parliaments and by introducing politically appointed judges and prosecutors who serve at the pleasure of the sitting majority. In Hungary, Viktor Orbán has used his majority to reduce citizens' rights and liberties – and has done so in the name of the people.

Ivan Krastev calls this "the paradox of Eastern Europe." We are in the rather grotesque situation in which those Central European voters who fought so hard for their freedom just thirty years ago are now voting for politicians campaigning to *eliminate* voters' own hard-won liberal rights!

Criticizing courts and justices and curtailing their power – at home and abroad – is now fashionable among populists in every corner of the world, from Brazil to the United States to Turkey, Russia, China, and Europe. In the EU, Hungary and Poland are not the only ones to have veered toward authoritarianism; their peers in the Czech Republic, together with Romanian[1] and Bulgarian governments, have also put the club's basic rule of law principles to the test.[2] Attacking judges and counter-majoritarian institutions resonates nicely with populists' general attack on liberal elites – a strategy that has been highly successful and continuously pursued in Britain under Boris Johnson as well.

According to Freedom House's yearly report, *Nations in Transit*, which measures democracy and the rule of law, however, Hungary recently registered "the largest cumulative decline in ... history, after its score has fallen for 10 consecutive years." And should no longer even be named a full democracy.[3]

But what exactly has happened? Hungary is an excellent example of how a democracy may die in silence, as Levitsky and Ziblatt present it in their book *How Democracies Die*.[4] As argued earlier in this book, it is also important to fully grasp how Hungary under Orbán's rule has not only gradually transformed Hungarian society itself but also strongly influenced our own classical conception of what a democracy is and should be. This has affected not only Hungary, Poland, and other struggling states, but – as just mentioned

– increasingly also the very way we discuss and define democracy in Europe and beyond. Two dimensions should be borne in mind apart from the paring back of the judiciary that I have already discussed. They symbolize what it means to bend the rules and move gradually in an authoritarian direction.

The first is a situation in which a democratically elected government uses its majority to limit pluralist media. The second is "gerrymandering," the bending of the electoral system so that party competition de facto no longer exists. We will now look at both of these in turn.

As an authoritarian leader, there are many other ways of cementing power besides contravening the most obvious rule of law principles. One well-known strategy also discussed above is to use governing majorities to limit freedom of speech, curtailing a free and critical press. When a government starts targeting journalists and criticism that it feels threaten it, this is the first sign of a "dying democracy," as Benjamin Carter Hett argues in his book *The Death of Democracy*.[5] Because few authoritarians tolerate criticism and investigative journalism that put them in a bad light, they often exploit their power to persecute critical media outlets. According to Hett, when Hitler came into power in the 1930s, overt censure and intimidation of political opponents were a daily occurrence. Attacking the press and other critical voices for being partisan, biased, and "politicizing" is a classic first step in undermining democracy.

We may think of this as something from the past, but intimidation and censure occur – according to my Hungarian sources – on a daily basis and have done so at an increasing speed for the past nine to ten years. As an article in the *Washington Post* reported after the successful reelection of Orbán and his Fidesz party in April 2018: "Viktor Orban promised 'revenge' against his enemies in Hungary. Now they're preparing for it."[6] The article cited threats to journalists from the well-known government spokesman Zoltán Kovács. It dealt with who, in his and the government's opinion, had the right to even comment on and intervene in politics after the election: "There's a legally elected and sovereign government ... When unelected people or organizations lobby or speak out against the government, that is basically against the country." This was a poorly disguised reference to the "unelected" journalists and civil society organizations who have started a habit of "interfering" in the government's work.

In societies that have lapsed into autocracy, control of the media and critical voices often becomes an obsession. The preoccupation with what the media writes in critical articles can even develop into an obsession, as we have seen with Donald Trump. Populist leaders, as mentioned, do not endure either critique or satire. If directly shutting down outspoken media looks too suspicious, outlets are bought up and their management staffed with pro-regime journalists and editors. This is what has happened to the critical print media in Hungary, where it has also become a common strategy to reserve photo permissions to journals with government-friendly coverage. Origo, for example, was once a critical news website revealing corruption and governmental fraud.[7] Today, "Origo is one of the prime minister's most dutiful media boosters, parroting his attacks on migrants and on George Soros, the

Hungarian-American philanthropist demonized by the far right on both sides of the Atlantic."[8]

For authoritarian regimes, attempting to control who gets media access is also essential. It is a question not only of getting your own message across to the public via campaigns and control of different outlets, but also of limiting the access of political opponents.

In Poland and particularly in Hungary, governments have recently shut down funding, withdrawn broadcasting and publication licenses, and bought up critical media to limit the outreach of critics independent of the government.[9] Orbán has, for instance, gathered all media companies under one large umbrella organization, KESMA,[10] which is regulated by the state and decides who can get broadcast permits and support. This has direct consequences for democracy: citizens are kept from learning the truth about government corruption and administrative failings, and competitors and opposition parties have no unbiased forums in which to debate views with the people in power.

Attacks on critics go beyond journalists and the free press. As already mentioned briefly above, the Hungarian-American philanthropist George Soros, who himself was born in a Jewish family in Hungary, announced in the spring of 2018 that he would move all of his activities from Hungary to Berlin. This happened not long after the general election of April 8, 2018, when the so-called "Soros law" was adopted. It criminalizes organizations (and external sponsors) who support NGOs providing help to undocumented immigrants. This is a prime example of identity politics in action. In campaigns on television, radio, and large billboards, Orbán describes migrants (who are almost exclusively portrayed as terrorists), Soros, and liberals as the enemies of the Hungarian people. Even Brussels and thus the EU – a core source of Orbán's family's own personal wealth – is consistently under attack.[11]

Soros has been attacked in many other ways as well. While democracies have always been prized for their promotion of free and critical universities, the one founded by George Soros – the internationally renowned Central European University (CEU) – has now been forced out of the country and moved large parts of its activities to Vienna. The Hungarian government has been bullying the CEU in various subtle ways for years, and in the spring of 2018 changed the requirements for operating a foreign university in Hungary. The CEU has tried its best to accommodate the constantly changing demands from the government; nonetheless, it has now been expelled. So for the first time in postwar history, a free European university has been forced to relocate due to harassment from a government which is also a member of the EU.[12] Few doubt that the pressure the university has suffered, and that in the end led it to move to Vienna, has its roots in Orbán's personal vendetta against George Soros. Viktor Orbán has spent millions in EU funds (!) posting anti-Semitic messages targeting Soros on billboards around the country, and it was, as mentioned earlier, only when the then EU Commission President Jean-Claude Juncker was subject to the same harassment that the conservatives in the European Parliament – a group to which Orbán's Fidesz party belongs – reacted.[13]

I would also like to touch on the Hungarian regime's gradual transformation of the electoral system, effected thanks to the governing Fidesz majority in three consecutive national elections. The objective has been clear: by changing the way electoral districts are drawn up, it has been possible to consolidate the regime and maximize electoral gains also in future.[14]

However, "gerrymandering," as it is called, is not the only creative amendment the Orbán government has implemented with its overwhelming majority.

When the Hungarian government won its first majority in 2010 it set itself immediately to amend the constitution, which has been changed a total of seven times, and more amendments are reportedly in store for 2020. Some of the changes have been about requiring public authorities to "honor Christian values" in everything they do. It has been about forbidding homelessness and forbidding people with another ethnic origin from ever settling in Hungary. It has also, however, been about limiting the right to assembly.[15] Moreover, since the government has largely taken control of the courts,[16] there have been few serious objections to these changes.[17] The electoral rules have now been transformed so radically that many foreign analysts doubt any opposition or political contender will ever have a serious chance of challenging the sitting majority.[18]

All this testifies to how vulnerable democracy is and how quickly it can falter. That European political leaders should have acted long ago was made clear in the Organization for Security and Co-operation in Europe (OSCE) report on the April 2018 national election. Observers on the ground testify that Hungary today is a free democracy in name only. Their report describes the election as: "characterized by a pervasive overlap between state and ruling party resources, undermining contestants' ability to compete on an equal basis." What does this mean in plain language? "Voters had a wide range of political options, but intimidating and xenophobic rhetoric, media bias and opaque campaign financing constricted the space for genuine political debate, hindering voters' ability to make a fully informed choice."[19] Orbán thus got 49 percent of the votes in the most recent election, but with his newly amended election laws, this yielded two-thirds of the seats in parliament for his party.

Numerous investigations further suggest that tribal rhetoric against Jews, migrants, the EU, and civil society organizations has functioned in part to hide the corruption surrounding Orbán and his family and friends. A lack of critical reporting has left the extent of this corruption unexamined, and fairly little is being written about it at present except for a few small internet media and in a few English-language and foreign-funded think tanks.[20] The government's continuing refusal to join the newly established European Prosecutor's Office has not helped. Despite the fact that Hungary receives the largest amount of EU funds per capita, Orbán's European colleagues have failed to demand this forcefully at any point.[21] The additional fact that the corruption reportedly involves misappropriation of EU funds makes a mockery of European taxpayers as well as other law-abiding member states. Fortunately, in its new "rule of law" strategy of July 2019, the Commission has proposed that member states that do not comply with the rule of law should be deprived of their EU funding. And while this sounds like something that should have been introduced a very long time ago, it is uncertain whether the heads of state or government will end up endorsing the proposal, even if the initiative is comprehensive – directed at all member states – and primarily will be about *protecting* the EU budget.

In discussions of civil society, one could easily confuse Orbán with Erdoğan or Putin: their views on others' right to speak up are nearly indistinguishable and NGOs, since they are not elected by the people, are not considered legitimate players. This is the clear experience of Marta Pardavi, Co-Chair of the Hungarian Helsinki group: "In [the Hungarian government's] view, civil society is not elected, so it has no right to have a say in politics."[22]

According to German-American sociologist Jan-Werner Müller, Hungarian civil society is on the verge of collapse and desperately needs help. The question today is, however, whether this help is available – and where. According to Müller we should start refusing Orbán's self-labeling as an "illiberal democrat." Orbán first used the term "illiberal democracy" in a speech at a youth camp in Transylvania in 2014, saying he refused to be subject to a so-called "Western" model of democracy.[23] The idea of the "Western model" is deeply questionable, however, and seems to serve largely as a smokescreen allowing Orbán to propose "alternative" democracy models that are "just as legitimate." If we follow along, however, we implicitly legitimize his regime and thus recognize that autocracies are in fact democracies. But let's make this clear: there *is* no such thing as an illiberal democracy. You are either a democrat who respects minorities, human rights, freedom of expression, the balance of powers, and a pluralistic and critical press, or you are not. Viktor Orbán's Hungary has already long ago crossed these red lines, moving beyond what can meaningfully be named a democracy in any real sense of the word.[24]

Why Liberals Are
Increasingly on
the Defensive, but
Shouldn't Be

Instead of apologizing for having been wrong, it is time for
internationalists to take the fight to an aging minority of
nativists and wall builders.

Charles Kenny, "The Bogus Backlash to Globalization"

In the fall of 2019, it was thirty years since the Berlin
Wall, which for forty years separated East and West
Germany, was dismantled. In the following years came
the velocity revolutions of the East and the Soviet
Union's final collapse. The euphoria was enormous
and the events are without doubt the greatest of my
generation. While this happened, most people were
convinced that these societal upheavals, and the enthu-
siasm in the East for finally becoming a part of a united
Europe, symbolized the ultimate victory of liberalism.
Europe could finally be healed and liberal democracy
outcompete all alternative state forms.

However, this was not how it would end. The tribal shift is instead challenging the liberal ideals that triumphed in the wake of the Second World War, and even more emphatically after the fall of Communism. Most believed, after 1989, that liberalism was the only game in town, and that old enmities had now finally been left behind. This was not just the opinion of Francis Fukuyama, who put forth this thesis in his bestselling book *The End of History and the Last Man*. Ordinary political scientists, journalists, and politicians were convinced as well. Particularly widespread was the conviction that rising wealth would automatically lead to support for democracy and a rejection of not only autocracy but also new wall-building and identity politics. The tribal tendencies I have described in this book show, however, that history can reverse and that many more people than we thought – even in the developed world – are charmed by authoritarian strongmen and tribalist rhetoric. Countless people no longer believe that democracy and the rule of law are worth fighting for, as Yascha Mounk states:

A quarter century ago, most citizens were proud to live in a liberal democracy and strongly rejected authoritarian alternatives to their system of government; now, many are growing increasingly hostile to democracy ... Over two-thirds of older Americans believe that it is extremely important to live in a democracy; among millennials, less than one-third do.[1]

Without wanting to sound alarmist, these are scary figures, and should warn us that our freedom and hard-won liberal institutions should never be taken for granted.

After the Brexit vote, the election of Donald Trump to the White House, and the rise of identitarian European populist movements, it has become fashionable among intellectuals and opinion leaders to engage in self-blame. A common narrative, now repeated ad nauseam, is that politicians and opinion makers were far too late to recognize (and understand) ordinary people's concerns and their longing for identity, a cultural sense of belonging, and the reinforcement of old – or, in the Catalan case, *new* – borders. I am *not* saying that people's worries shouldn't be taken seriously. They should. But it is important to understand the real causes of frustration and avoid jumping to easy conclusions.

Studies have shown that both Trump and Brexit voters were reacting to growing inequality as well as to issues of identity. Governments in many Western societies have failed to address the excessive accumulation of wealth among small sectors of society, which has left many ordinary people worse off economically than previous generations.[2] The absence of political will to deal effectively with corruption, tax fraud, or tax evasion, combined with a rash of outright financial speculation, has made many people angry.

But instead of realizing that more and not less European and global cooperation is needed to cope with these ills, many have thrown in the towel and opted for easy anti-globalist posturing. They want us to believe the real problems are not financial speculation, corruption, and the Russian-American attempts to foment anger against the EU, but rather Western elites, international institutions, and liberal values in general. When we play into these anti-globalism deceptions, we are however not helping to solve current challenges, but heedlessly parroting Trump, Putin, and the Russian-sponsored extreme right. The Austrian right-wing national FPÖ party, which in 2019 demonstrated its willingness to sell Austria's largest newspaper (and grant major building contracts) to the Russians, for support and positive publicity in the same newspaper, is a good example of how corruption and liberal sellout are currently at the heart of all of Europe.

And yet we hear many argue that all liberals should bow in shame and recognize that the people have had it and should be allowed to cut themselves off from the world. This attitude is, however, naïve, cowardly, and dangerous.[3] It glorifies a past that no longer exists, pulls away from responsibility to the rest of the world and for future generations, and legitimizes replacing politics with identitarianism. If the liberal order is to be saved, we must not only challenge such ideas but also be open to dialogue, critique, and compromise.[4] We must insist that democracy should be based on *principles* irreducible to the tribe or even the individual nation-state.

However, as Fukuyama has recently pointed out,[5] identity politics and tribal thinking do not belong only to the right wing. In many democracies, the left is more interested in promoting special interests than in contributing to common solutions to collective challenges. On the right, however, one exists inside the identarian bubble, where, according to Fukuyama, national or regional identity is often directly linked to discussions of ethnicity, religion – and sometimes even race. In Europe today, this means that we are facing a major threat: the gradual termination of our own humanistic and inclusive liberal heritage. What do I mean by that?

I believe it has not yet occurred to us that our way of life as we have known it since the Second World War and now take for granted – with the freedom to speak out and live in inclusive and tolerant rule of law societies – are in danger. Europe is a shrinking continent surrounded by autocracies and authoritarian leaders, so who says that precisely our values will be the ones to win the global battle in the decades to come? If we dare not even defend these at home as well as at the European level, this will hardly happen.

Thus, we need to not only stick together in Europe, but also stand up for the worldview and values of the Enlightenment if we want the EU to play a role on the world stage in the decades to come. Our opponents are not only the identitarians among us but global giants and countries like China, the US, India, Turkey, and Brazil. A few years ago, the UN made a forecast of population development in the world. It shows some rather unsettling figures for how the EU will develop in the coming decades. With Europeans constituting 22 percent of the earth's population in 1950 and 11 percent in 2010, by 2050 we will only make up 8 percent of the planet's population. By 2100 we are down to 6 percent. Thus, only 6 percent of the world's population will be European. There is, in other words, no guarantee that it will be *us* who will end up influencing the rest of the world with our values and rules, as we have done for centuries. Not only in terms of trade and economics, but also when it comes to international law, democracy, human rights, environment, consumer security, and climate. The moral here is, of course, that if we cannot even agree to preserve our values within Europe and to do it together, how can we expect it to be our and not the Chinese rules and norms that will dominate the world for our children and grandchildren?

As for the economy and the opportunity to influence the world and the way we trade with each other, Michel Barnier, the EU's Brexit Chief Negotiator, makes a good point. In the spring of 2019 in Copenhagen, with this "shrink thesis" in mind, he pointed out how big a difference there will be in whether the EU is moving forward together as one bloc, or as individual countries. Where Britain, Germany, and France were part of the G8 (largest industrialized states) in 2016, figures from the UN and the EU show that only Germany will remain one of the world's eight largest and most influential economies in 2050. Both the UK and France will be out of the G8, and the world's dominant powers would instead consist of (1) China, (2) the United States, (3) India, (4) Indonesia, (5) Japan, (6) Brazil, (7) Germany, and (8) Mexico. If, on the other hand, the EU acts as *one* unified bloc, by 2050 we would continue to be the fourth strongest economy, after China, the United States, and India.

Although some might legitimately object that it is time for Europeans to give way to other world powers, most of us would probably still prefer it to be a world governed by liberal values, rules, and democracy rather than autocracy we leave to our children, our grandchildren, and their children. Would anyone call this a kind of rebirth of complacent imperialism? Perhaps, but I have yet to meet a (non-brainwashed) person on this planet who would not always prefer democracy and liberal values to autocracy – were they to be given a real choice.

It is evident that Europe, more than ever, needs to insist that democracy and the rule of law as well as a rule-based market economy are what we should aspire to in the future. It is, however, by no means certain it will succeed. But if we don't fight for it – and aren't aware that it only has a chance to succeed if we stand together rather than hide behind new high walls and borders – the race is lost in advance.

Concluding Remarks

In the introduction to this book, I pose the question whether we are facing a generalized tribalization in Europe today. The answer, I have argued, depends on where we look and whether we are willing to face our own tribal demons. It should be clear by now that tribalist currents are now universal, and go beyond Brexit, Catalan separatism, and backlashing Eastern states, with their embrace of identitarian values. Tribalism is deeper, and has crept into all corners of our language, influencing even the very way we think about democracy.

Many of those who used to defend the twin pillars of democracy – a free press and independent representative institutions – are now so afraid of accusations of political correctness and of taking the moral "high ground" that they have started confessing their sins as former promoters of tolerance and liberal values. They instead write long essays or books about how wrong they were and how they regret failing to grasp why people voted for Trump, right-wing populist or separatist parties, or Brexit.[1] Instead of insisting on the truth, that liberal democracy is the best thing we have, they implicitly defend a return to cultural exclusion and describe the current populist rage as a "natural" and understandable reaction.[2] In refusing to defend the rule-based European and international order we have relied on for the past seventy years, they, however, thereby help legitimize a tribal agenda and unwittingly lend support to people like Trump and Putin, who have an explicit wish to see Europe dissolve.

The unwillingness to defend our values represents a new form of relativism or misunderstood tolerance, in which politicians, scholars, and intellectuals no longer dare to distinguish right from wrong or a true democracy from a false one. We no longer even insist that democracy is completely hollow without the rule of law and counter-majoritarian institutions, as it may upset those who think differently. Insisting on what is right doesn't fit the new tribalist megatrend where the powerful majority, it is suggested, are always right.

When Orbán or Kaczyński fire judges, co-opt or eliminate the free press, or change electoral rules to immunize themselves against competing views, most stay silent or argue that these strongmen were elected, and so their actions are legitimate and even democratic. As a comment on this development, Hungarian law professor Gábor Halmai, together with colleagues like Dan Kelemen and Laurent Pech, has forcefully argued that Western intellectuals and thinkers have in fact helped and thus legitimized Eastern autocrats by promoting the idea of "legal pluralism" and "constitutional tolerance."[3] By arguing that we in Europe should respect a "diversity of constitutions" and ways of being a democracy, postmodern legal theorists have – unintentionally – provided the theoretical basis for illiberalism. We have moreover become so afraid of speaking up – in particular to Orbán, Kaczyński, and Babiš – that in order to accommodate our own feelings of guilt for having been "on the right side of the wall" while Eastern Europeans were suffering, we are en route to killing liberal democracy. This is, however, a devastating misunderstanding that, if cultivated further, will harm any attempt to truly transform hybrid regimes into livable democracies.

As our rule-based order falls apart – whether we look at trade, security, human rights, or democracy – the defenders of the liberal world order and the EU have largely silenced themselves. However, if you silence yourself you are sleepwalking into the abyss, just as the good soldier Švejk naïvely marched into the Great War in 1914.[4]

Identity political tribalism is dangerous because it is deceptive and erodes the very courage to speak up against it. By selling itself, often successfully, as anti-elitism and the voice of the people, while at the same time abusing public funds and agitating for constitutional tolerance, it has managed to disarm many proponents of "the open society," as Karl Popper argued back in 1945.[5] This point is also made eloquently by the Slovenian philosopher Slavoj Žižek. Žižek argues that populists and their mainstream followers have intimidated and discredited liberals so effectively that many have begun to backpedal on the very ideals they were raised to believe in. They have lost their way, their confidence and trust in the liberal democracy that the West not only used to cherish, but even – admittedly with

Concluding Remarks

mixed success – tried to promote elsewhere as a value possessed of universal legitimacy. However, the failure to convince others of the virtues of liberal democracy and free speech hopefully doesn't delegitimize these values themselves.

While tribal demagogues won the hearts and minds of many Europeans, leaving fewer and fewer defenders of European core values, they have pigeonholed those who continue to believe in joint European solutions as naïve, elitist cosmopolitans. The liberal elite, we are told, not only want open borders for mass immigration; they also embrace globalization while ruthlessly squeezing all those who have fallen behind. Worse still, they arrogantly impose liberal values on others who prefer internal borders, cultural particularism, and even authoritarian leaders and illiberalism.⁶ Why is liberalism even better than illiberalism, they would like to ask their smug liberal friends.⁷ Few today dare to raise their voice in an answer. The liberal West has become afraid of its own shadow.

This book is not a plea for a return to a Europe that naïvely believed in its own superiority. But if we want to continue living in an open society, we should never accept double standards for democracy. Nor should we hide behind identities that delegitimize criticism and debate and limit the possibility of collaboration and compromise.

Notes

Introduction

1 See A.M. Slaughter, "A Real New World Order," *Foreign Affairs*, 76 (1997).

2 F. Fukuyama, *The End of History and the Last Man*, Free Press, 1992.

3 The Varieties of Democracy (V-Dem) project is directed by Staffan Lindberg from Gothenburg University in Sweden. Through its V-Dem index, it examines the state of democracy in the world, using seven different democratic forms. The data I refer to here are from the 2018 report. See a summary of the findings in S.I. Lindberg, "The Nature of Democratic Backsliding in Europe," *Carnegie Europe*, July 24, 2018.

4 See W.G. Sumner, *Folkways: A Study of Mores, Manners, Customs and Morals*, Dover Publications, 2002, p. 13.

5 *The Economist*, "The New Political Divide: Farewell, Left Versus Right. The Contest that Matters Now Is Open Against Closed," July 30, 2016.

Notes to pp. 8–14

6 See the revealing coverage by Selam Gebrekidan, Matt Apuzzo, and Benjamin Novak in "The Money Farmers: How Oligarchs and Populists Milk the E.U. for Millions," *The New York Times*, November 3, 2019, https://www.nytimes.com/2019/11/03/world/europe/eu-farm-subsidy-hungary.html.
7 See E. Rosenbach, "The Catalan Independence Referendum is a Smokescreen for Other Issues," *Independent*, October 1, 2017.
8 Harriet Agerholm, "Denmark Uses Controversial 'Jewellery Law' to Seize Assets from Refugees for First Time," *Independent*, July 1, 2016, https://www.independent.co.uk/news/world/europe/denmark-jewellery-law-migrants-refugees-asylum-seekers-unhcr-united-nations-a7113056.html.

Imagined Communities and Identity Politics
1 B. Anderson, *Imagined Communities: Reflections on the Origin and Spread of Nationalism*, Verso, 1991.
2 Uffe Østergaard, "Why Globalism Cannot Extinguish the Feeling of National Belonging" (in Danish), October 2, 2016, https://videnskab.dk/kultur-samfund/nation (my translation from Danish). See also his *Hvorhen Europa?*, Djøf, 2018.
3 E. Weber, *Peasants into Frenchmen: The Modernization of Rural France 1870–1914*, Stanford University Press, 1976.
4 J.H.H. Weiler, "Secessionism and Its Discontents," in C. Closa (ed.), *Secession from a Member State and Withdrawal from the European Union*, Cambridge University Press, 2017, p. 26.

5 See A. Chua, "Tribal World," *Foreign Affairs*, July/ August 2018.

6 See S. Schackle, "The Problem with Identity Politics: Q&A with Asad Haider," *New Humanist*, July 13, 2018.

7 See J. Macwhirter, "'Quislings, Collaborators and Traitors!' British MEP Attacks Remainers for Stalling Brexit," *Express*, May 31, 2018.

8 See T. Garton Ash, "Liberal Europe Isn't Dead Yet. But its Defenders Face a Long Hard Struggle," *The Guardian*, July 9, 2018.

9 See Chua, "Tribal World." Her recent, commendable book is A. Chua, *Political Tribes: Group Instinct and the Fate of Nations*, Penguin, 2018.

10 See A. Adonis, "Traitors? No, the Lords are the Voice of Reason on Brexit," *The New European*, April 21, 2018.

11 A good example is Michael Gove defending British identity politics in a speech in Westminster on May 21, 2018. See comments on Gove's "identitarian" speech in N. Malik, "Gove's 'Identitarian' Speech Shows How Toxic He Has Become," *The Guardian*, May 22, 2018.

12 Today Spanish is taught as a foreign language in Catalan state schools, which means two hours a week in elementary school and three hours a week in secondary school, the same as English. See P. Álvarez, "Spanish Government Plans to End 'Catalan-Only' School Language Policy," *El Pais*, February 16, 2018.

13 Here cited in A. Wong, "Is Catalonia Using Schools as a Political Weapon?" *The Atlantic*, November 3, 2017.

Tribal Thinking and Dreams of Detachment

1 See the Teller Report, "The Complicity of the Rectors of Catalan Universities Chronicles the University Revolt," 30 October, 2019, https://www.tellerreport.com/news/2019-10-30---the-complicity-of-the-rectors-of-catalan-universities-chronicles-the-university-revolt-.BkjEJdI9B.html.
2 B. Anderson, *Imagined Communities: Reflections on the Origin and Spread of Nationalism*, Verso, 1991, p. 46. See also H. Miller and K. Miller, "Language Policy and Identity: The Case of Catalonia," *International Studies in Sociology of Education*, 6:1 (1996).
3 E. Kedourie, *Nationalism*, Hutchinson, 1960, p. 63.
4 See F. Ortiz, "Catalan Language Revival Fuels Backlash in Spain," *Reuters*, July 14, 2014.
5 Of the 2,286,217 million voters who cast a ballot, 92.01 percent voted for independence, on a turnout of 43 percent. See Wikipedia, "2017 Catalan Independence Referendum," https://en.wikipedia.org/wiki/2017_Catalan_independence_referendum.
6 C. Fasone, "Secession and the Ambiguous Place of Regions Under EU Law," in C. Closa (ed.), *Secession from a Member State and Withdrawal from the European Union*, Cambridge University Press, 2017.
7 Fasone "Secession."
8 Fasone, "Secession."
9 J.H.H. Weiler, "Secessionism and Its Discontents" in Closa, *Seccession from a Member State*, p. 18.
10 T.R. Monés, "The Lies of Catalan Separatism Are a Threat to Europe," *Politico*, March 10, 2018.
11 Fasone, "Secession," p. 56.

12 Fasone "Secession," p. 54.
13 Council of the European Union, "History," https://www.consilium.europa.eu/en/history/?filters=2031.
14 See the letter of J.M. Barroso, October 10, 2012, to the UK House of Lords.
15 See the convincing argument by the Canadian Supreme Court on Quebec's possible secession from Canada 1998, indexed as "Reference re Secession of Quebec."
16 Weiler, "Secessionism and Its Discontents."

Why Brexit is Just Another Kind of Tribalism
1 See https://www.youtube.com/watch?v=dNpcNNGapDs.
2 See A. Appelbaum, "Is This the End of the West as We Know It?" *Washington Post*, March 4, 2016.
3 Very telling about the EU's diminishing interest in the British "mess" was the June 2018 EU Summit, where less than four (!) minutes were devoted to Brexit, despite there still being no plan so far for how the UK would leave. And this was hardly unusual. The British Prime Minister again and again came empty handed to Council meetings in 2017 and 2018, close to the end of negotiations. This lack of engagement is endemic: former Brexit Minister David Davis is said to have spent fewer than four hours in Brussels negotiating the country's exit in 2017. See K. Hopps, "EU Summit 2018: Where is David Davis? Is Brexit Secretary at European Council Meeting?" *Express*, June 28, 2018.
4 See A. Massie, "Brexit Has Become England's White Whale," *The Spectator*, June 19, 2018.

5 E. Ross (2019), "Is Brexit Worth Scotland's Independence?" *The Atlantic*, August 1, 2019, https://www.theatlantic.com/international/ archive/2019/08/scottish-independence-and-brexit/595234. See also BBC News, "Will Brexit Break Britain, and Would England Care?" July 23, 2019, https://www.bbc.com/news/uk-scotland-49053233.

6 See K. Debeuf, "Is a World War Coming 100 Years After the First?" *The Hill*, November 12, 2018. See also K. Debeuf, *Tribalization: Why War Is Coming*, ASP, 2018.

7 T. Snyder, *The Road to Unfreedom*, Penguin, 2018.

8 See Radio Free Europe/Radio Liberty, "EU Official Names Russia as Main Disrupter of Elections in Europe," November 14, 2018.

9 See L. Mälksoo, "Strasbourg's Effect on Russia – and Russia's Effect on Strasbourg," *Völkerechtsblog*, January 3, 2018.

The Tribal Shift in Central and Eastern Europe

1 I. Krastev, *After Europe*, University of Pennsylvania Press, 2017.

2 See I. Krastev, "Central Europe is a Lesson to Liberals: Don't Be Anti-Nationalist," *The Guardian*, July 11, 2018.

3 Selam Gebrekidan, Matt Apuzzo, and Benjamin Novak in "The Money Farmers: How Oligarchs and Populists Milk the E.U. for Millions," *The New York Times*, November 3, 2019, https://www.nytimes.com/2019/11/03/world/europe/eu-farm-subsidy-hungary.html.

4 D. Waldner and E. Lust, "Unwelcome Change:

Coming to Terms with Democratic Backsliding," *Annual Review of Political Science*, 21 (2018).

5 See J. Diamant and S. Gardner, "In EU, There's an East–West Divide Over Religious Minorities, Gay Marriage, National Identity," *Pew Research Center*, October 19, 2018.

6 See European Commission, "European Neighbourhood Policy and Enlargement Negotiations: Accession Criteria," https://ec.europa.eu/neighbourhood-enlargement/policy/glossary/terms/accession-criteria_en.

7 P. Lendvai, *Orbán: Hungary's Strongman*, Oxford University Press, 2018.

8 One third of the member states or the Commission, after consulting the European Parliament, can recommend this. The procedure needs the backing of three quarters of the member states. If, after the proceedings, the member state does not amend its laws, the European Council can unanimously suspend the country's voting rights.

9 See European Parliament, "Motion for a European Parliament Resolution," in the Sargentini Report, July 4, 2018.

10 It should be mentioned that the EPP Spitzenkandidat election in November 2018 was between a hardliner when it comes to fundamental rights, former Finish Prime Minister Alexander Stubb, and Manfred Weber, a CSU member and longtime friend of Orbán, as already mentioned. Weber won the nomination with an 80 percent majority at a party congress in Helsinki.

11 See the analysis by H. Grabbe and S. Lehne, "Defending EU Values in Poland and Hungary," *Carnegie Europe*, September 4, 2017.

12 This was the case with Austria back in 2000 when EU leaders isolate the Austrian government because it let the right-wing FPÖ join the government.
13 See M. Ramgotra, "Can Democracy Vote Itself Out of Existence?" *The Conversation*, July 16, 2018.
14 See J.W. Müller, "The Problem With 'Illiberal Democracy,'" *Social Europe*, January 27, 2016.

Who Cares About Democracy?
1 See R. Bellamy, *Political Constitutionalism: A Republican Defence of the Constitutionality of Democracy*, Cambridge University Press, 2007. See also R. Hirschl, *Towards Juristocracy: The Origins and Consequences of the New Constitutionalism*, Harvard University Press, 2004.
2 James Fearon and David Laitan, "Ethnicity, Insurgency, and Civil War," *American Political Science Review*, 97 (2003).
3 *The Economist*, "After Decades of Triumph Democracy Is Losing Ground," June 14, 2018.
4 See *The Economist*, citing Pew Research Centre, June 18, 2018.
5 Amanda Taub, "How Stable Are Democracies? 'Warning Signs Are Flashing Red,'" *The New York Times*, November 29, 2016, https://www.nytimes.com/2016/11/29/world/americas/western-liberal-democracy.html. See also Yascha Mounk and Roberto Foa, "The Signs of Deconsolidation," *Journal of Democracy*, 28:1 (2017).
6 Mounk and Foa, "The Signs of Deconsolidation," p. 6.
7 See *Economist* "After Decades of Triumph." See also Y. Mounk, *The People vs. Democracy: Why*

Our Freedom Is in Danger and How to Save It, Harvard University Press, 2018.

8 See M. Collins, "The Pros And Cons of Globalization," *Forbes*, May 6, 2015.

9 See S. Illing, "Why Trump's Populist Appeal Is about Culture, Not the Economy," *Vox*, March 27, 2017. See also P. Norris and R. Englehart, *Cultural Backlash: Trump, Brexit and the Rise of Authoritarian-Populism*, Cambridge University Press, 2018.

10 Retrieved from Fairvote, "Voter Turnout," https://www.fairvote.org/voter_turnout#voter_turnout_101.

11 See A. Solijonov, *Voter Turnout Trends around the World*, Stockholm, 2016.

12 J.H. Nielsen and M.N. Franklin, *The Eurosceptic 2014 European Parliament Elections: Second Order or Second Rate?*, Palgrave Macmillan, 2017. See also C. Bischoff and M. Wind, "Denmark" and "Sweden," in D.M. Viola (ed.), *Routledge Handbook of European Elections*, Routledge, 2015.

13 S. Hix and C. Lord, *Political Parties in the European Union*, Palgrave Macmillan, 1997, pp. 87–90.

Who Are the People?

1 C. Rostbøll, "Catalonia and Europe at a Crossroads for Democracy? Debate with Carles Puigdemont," unpublished paper, 2018.

2 See A. MacDowall, "Voters Back Viktor Orbán's Rejection of EU Migrant Quotas," *Politico*, February 10, 2016.

3 See K. Rogoff, "Britain's Democratic Failure," *Project Syndicate*, June 21, 2016.

The Purpose of a Consitution

1 See United Nations General Assembly, "Declaration on Principles of International Law Concerning Friendly Relations and Co-Operation Among States in Accordance with the Charter of the United Nations," October 24, 1970.

2 All Spanish regions base their authority on the constitution of 1978. It was adopted during the period of democratic transition from the Franco regime to democratic rule.

3 In 2017 the steepest score declines in Western Europe were recorded by Malta (−0.24), Spain (−0.22), Turkey (−0.16), and France (−0.12). At 8.08, Spain's score remains just above the threshold for full democracies. See Economist Intelligence Unit, "The Democracy Index World Table 2006–2017," in *Democracy Index 2017*, pp. 13–17, https://www.eiu.com/public/topical_report.aspx?campaignid=DemocracyIndex2017.

4 See A.G. Munoz, "Catalan Independence in the Spanish Constitution and Courts," *OUPblog*, November 6, 2017. See also Library of Congress, "Spain: Constitutional Court Finds Catalonia Sovereignty Declaration Unconstitutional," April 24, 2014.

5 See J. G. Oliva, "The Troubling Legal and Political Uncertainty Facing Catalonia," *Social Europe*, February 20, 2018.

6 See Oliva "Troubling Legal and Political Uncertainty."

7 C. Mudde and C.R. Kaltwasser, "Populism," in M. Freeden and M. Stears (eds.), *The Oxford Handbook of Ideologies*, Oxford University Press.

8 Larry Diamond, "Yes, Dictators are Ascendant: But People All Over the World Are Fighting Back," *Washington Post*, July 21, 2019.

Democracy Without Limits?

1 Alexis de Tocqueville, *Democracy in America and Two Essays on America*, trans Gerald E. Bevan, intro. and notes Isaac Kramnick, Penguin, 2003, p. 314.
2 The Magna Carta of 1215 was the first edict challenging the authority of the English king, forcing him to accept the rule of law (as a limit to his power), and protecting the people from feudal abuse.
3 M. Wind, *International Courts and Domestic Politics*, Cambridge University Press, 2018. See also M. Wind and J.H.H. Weiler, *European Constitutionalism Beyond the State*, Cambridge University Press, 2003.
4 M. Rask Madsen and J. Christoffersen, *The European Court of Human Rights between Law and Politics*, Oxford University Press, 2011.
5 M. Shapiro and A. Stone Sweet, *On Law, Politics, and Judicialization*, Oxford University Press, 2002.
6 Shapiro and Stone Sweet, *On Law, Politics, and Judicialization*, p. 136.
7 See *The Economist*, "Poland's Ruling Law and Justice Party Is Doing Lasting Damage," April 21, 2018, p. 23. The work of R.D. Kelemen, K. Scheppele, and L. Perch has eminently covered the Eastern European democratic setback. See R.D. Kelemen, "Europe's Other Democratic Deficit: National Authoritarianism in Europe's

Democratic Union," *Government and Opposition*, 52:2 (2017).

8 Likely to the surprise of some, several well-functioning democracies, among them the Nordic ones, have long survived without the practice of active judicial review. In Sweden and Finland, it was even constitutionally illegal for courts to exercise judicial review until the 1990s, and in Denmark, the country's highest court has only once in 180 years set aside a parliamentary statute. More in M. Wind, "Do Scandinavians Care About International Law?" *Nordic Journal of International Law*, 85:4 (2016). See also M. Scheinin, *Constitutionalism and the Welfare State: Constitutional Perspectives*, Norden, 2001.

9 See M. Wind and J.E. Rytter, "In Need of Juristocracy?" *International Journal of Constitutional Law*, 9:2 (2011). See also Wind, "Do Scandinavians Care About International Law?"

10 See European Court of Human Rights, "Brighton Final Declaration," April 2012. See also Committee of Ministers of the Council of Europe, "Copenhagen Declaration," April 2018.

11 Speech by T. May at Lancaster House, January 17, 2017.

12 For more see Owen Bowcott, Ben Quinn, and Severin Carrell, "Johnson's Suspension of Parliament Unlawful, Supreme Court Rules," *The Guardian*, September 24, 2019, https://www.theguardian.com/law/2019/sep/24/boris-johnsons-suspension-of-parliament-unlawful-supreme-court-rules-prorogue.

13 I. Krastev, *After Europe*, University of Pennsylvania Press, 2017, p. 71.

14 Judicial independence is fundamental to the separation of powers as Montesquieu describes it in *The Spirit of the Laws* (1748). Judicial independence is a key element in most democratic constitutions and formally endorsed at the international level in the United Nations General Assembly's Basic Principles on the Independence of the Judiciary.

15 See R. Dworkin, "The Moral Reading of the Constitution," *The New York Review of Books*, March 21, 1996.

16 See A. Brzozowzki, "Commission Starts Procedure Against Poland Over Supreme Court Overhaul," *Euractiv*, July 2, 2018. On article 7 see European Commission. "Rule of Law: European Commission Acts to Defend Judicial Independence in Poland," December 20, 2017.

17 One of these is that PiS has placed loyal government supporters in the council that appoints new judges. The government has recently (April 2019) relentlessly pursued its course and established a new disciplinary system to punish judges who judge in a way that the political majority does not welcome, or who do as the judges of the EU treaties must, namely submit cases they have doubts about to the European Court of Justice. For more, see Alice Tidey, "EU Moves to Sanction Poland over Law Targeting Judges," *Euronews*, April 4, 2019, https://www.euronews.com/2019/04/04/eu-moves-to-sanction-poland-over-law-targeting-judges.

18 See the legal order issued by the European Court in October 2018, C-619/18, Commission v. Poland. See the verdict in BBC News, "Poland Reinstates Supreme Court Judges Following EU Ruling,"

December 17, 2018. See also C. Davies, "Hostile Takeover: How Law and Justice Captured Poland's Courts," Freedom House, May 2018.

19 See S. Sierakowski, "How Poland Could Return to the EU Fold," *New Europe*, November 27, 2018.

20 See the outline above of the Copenhagen criteria.

21 Frans Timmermans, "Remarks by First Vice-President Frans Timmermans on Further Strengthening of the Rule of Law in the EU," April 3, 2019, https:// ec.europa.eu/commission/presscorner/detail/en/ SPEECH_19_1972.

22 See S. Kuvaldin, "No Extradition to Poland," *Legal Dialogue*, July 12, 2017. See also P. Smyth and C. Keena, "EU Court Backs Irish Judge's Right to Query Polish Justice System," *The Irish Times*, July 25, 2018.

23 See Kelemen "Europe's Other Democratic Deficit."

24 V. Orbán, speech at Bálványos Free Summer University and Youth Camp in Transylvania, July 26, 2014.

Are Illiberal Democracies Democracies?

1 See *The Financial Times*, "Romania Has Joined the Retreat from Rule of Law," October 4, 2018.

2 BTA Bulgarian News Agency, "Bulgarian Judges Association Support Judge Panov for His Speech in MEDEL Conference," November 27, 2018. See also European Parliament, "Rule of Law: In Romania Independence of the Judiciary Is Up for Debate in Plenary," October 2018.

3 Freedom House, *Nations in Transit 2018: Confronting Illiberalism*, 2018.

4 See S. Levitsky and D. Ziblatt, *How Democracies Die*, Penguin, 2018.

5 B. C. Hett, *The Death of Democracy*, Penguin, 2018.
6 See G. Witte "Viktor Orban Promised 'Revenge' Against His Enemies in Hungary. Now They're Preparing for It," *The Washington Post*, May 15, 2018.
7 See P. Kingsley and B. Novak, "The Website That Shows How a Free Press Can Die," *The New York Times*, November 24, 2018.
8 See Kingsley and Novak, "Website."
9 All of this has been well reported by Freedom House, "Freedom on the Net 2017: Hungary Country Profile."
10 The official English name is the Central European Press and Media Foundation.
11 Andras Petho, "Hungary: While Orban Attacks EU, His Brother Gets Funds," September 6, 2016, https://www.occrp.org/en/27-ccwatch/cc-watch-briefs/5614-hungary-while-hungary-s-pm-attacks-brussels-his-brother-s-company-gets-money-from-the-eu. See also Selam Gebrekidan, Matt Apuzzo, and Benjamin Novak in "The Money Farmers: How Oligarchs and Populists Milk the E.U. for Millions," *The New York Times*, November 3, 2019, https://www.nytimes.com/2019/11/03/world/europe/eu-farm-subsidy-hungary.html.
12 See C. Patricolo, "CEU Formally Moves from Budapest to Vienna," *Emerging Europe*, October 26, 2018.
13 See Witte "Viktor Orban." Two Hungarian journalists undercover contributed to this article in *The Washington Post*.
14 See N. Schackow, "Hungary's Changing Electoral

System: Reform or Repression Inside the European Union?" conference paper, ResearchGate, April 2014.

15 Hungarian Civil Liberties Union, "Hungary's 7-Year-Old Constitution Is Amended for the 7th Time," *Liberties*, June 28, 2018, https://www. liberties.eu/en/news/hungarian-fundamental-law-has-been-amended-7-times-by-the-parliament-since-2011/15237. See also Orange Files, "Campaign Caravan," *The Orange Files: Notes on Illiberal Democracy in Hungary*, May 26, 2019, https:// theorangefiles.hu.

16 See Z. Fleck, "Judges Under Attack in Hungary," *Verfassungsblog*, May 14, 2018. See also B. Novak and P. Kingsley, "Hungary's Judges Warn of Threats to Judicial Independence," *The New York Times*, May 2, 2018.

17 Viktor Orbán's latest innovation is a parallel court system consisting entirely of political appointees, which will bypass the existing courts – though they too are almost completely controlled by the government. See K. Than, "Hungary to Set Up Courts Overseen Directly by Government," Reuters, December 12, 2018.

18 See K. Verseck, "Orbán Cements his Power with New Voting Law," *Spiegel*, October 30, 2012. See also Z. Csaky, "The End of Viktor Orban's Peacock Dance," *Foreign Policy*, September 14, 2018.

19 See OSCE, "Overlap of State and Ruling Party Resources Undermines Contestants' Ability to Compete on Equal Basis in Hungary Elections, OSCE/ ODIHR Observers Say," April 9, 2018, https:// www.osce.org/odihr/elections/hungary/377404.

20 See European Parliament, "Corruption and Misuse of EU Funds in Hungary," July 26, 2018.
21 See M. Becker, P. Müller, C. Schult, and J. Puhl, "EU Considers Funding Cuts for Eastern Europe," *Spiegel*, April 4, 2018.
22 See Witte "Viktor Orbán."
23 V. Orbán, speech at Bálványos Free Summer University and Youth Camp in Transylvania, July 26, 2014.
24 See J-W. Müller, "'Democracy' Still Matters," *The New York Times*, April 5, 2018.

Why Liberals Are Increasingly on the Defensive, But Shouldn't Be

1 Y. Mounk, *The People vs. Democracy: Why Our Freedom is in Danger and How to Reverse It*, Harvard University Press, 2018.
2 See *The Economist*, "For Richer for Poorer," October 13, 2012. See also C. Pazzanese, "The Costs of Inequality: Increasingly, It's the Rich and the Rest," *The Harvard Gazette*, February 8, 2016.
3 See A. Chua, "Tribal World," *Foreign Affairs*, July/August 2018.
4 This is a point made eloquently by C. Rostbøll in C. Rostbøll and T. Scavenius, *Compromise and Disagreement in Contemporary Political Theory*, Routledge, 2018.
5 F. Fukuyama, "Against Identity Politics: The New Tribalism and the Crisis of Democracy," *Foreign Affairs*, October 2018.

Concluding Remarks

1 E. Luce, *The Retreat of the Western Liberalism*, Atlantic Monthly Press, 2017, is a good example.

2 See M. Lilla "The End of Identity Liberalism," *The New York Times*, November 18 2016. See also T. Stanley "Liberals Should Blame Themselves for Their Decline – They Got So Much Wrong," *The Telegraph*, September 3, 2016.

3 Gábor Halmai, *Abuse of Constitutional Identity. The Hungarian Constitutional Court on Interpretation of Article E (2) of the Fundamental Law*, Working Paper, European University Institute, Florence, 2018, https://cadmus.eui.eu/handle/1814/60037. For a similar brilliant argument see R. Daniel Kelemen and Laurent Pech, *Why Autocrats Love Constitutional Identity and Constitutional Pluralism: Lessons from Hungary and Poland*, Working Paper No. 2, Reconnect, https://reconnect-europe.eu/wp-content/uploads/2018/10/RECONNECT-WorkingPaper2-Kelemen-Pech-LP-KO.pdf.

4 J. Hašek, *The Good Soldier Švejk*, Penguin, 2016. See also C. Clark, *The Sleepwalkers: How Europe Went to War in 1914*, Allen Lane, 2012. See also K. Debeuf, *Tribalization: Why War is Coming*, ASP, 2018.

5 K. Popper, *The Open Society and Its Enemies*, 2 vols, Routledge (1945).

6 See J-W. Müller, "The Problem with 'Illiberal Democracy'," *Social Europe*, January 27, 2016.

7 See C. Fridersdorf, "What Critiques of 'Smug Liberals' Miss," *The Atlantic*, May 3, 2017.